Runes for

Beginners:

A Pagan Guide to Reading and Casting the
Elder Futhark Rune Stones for Divination,
Norse Magic and Modern Witchcraft

Melissa Gomes

RUNES FOR BEGINNERS: A Pagan Guide to Reading and Casting the Elder Futhark Rune Stones for Divination, Norse Magic and Modern Witchcraft

by Melissa Gomes

TABLE OF CONTENTS

BONUS 1: FREE WORKBOOK - VALUE

~~12.99$~~

To help you take some time for yourself and reflect on what actions to take while reading the book, I have prepared a Free Workbook with some key questions to ask yourself and a To Do List which can help you get deeper into the topic of this book. I hope this helps!

VISIT THE FOLLOWING LINK:

>> https://swiy.io/RunesWB<<

OR scan the QR Code with your phone's camera

BONUS 2: FREE BOOK – VALUE $14.99

As a way of saying thank you for downloading this book, I'm offering the eBook *ASATRU FOR BEGINNERS* for FREE.

In *Runes for Beginners*, Melissa Gomes reveals some of the most interesting and secret aspects of how to perform Runes Reading and Runes Casting. You will discover new insights into the magical word of Runes and how to link with them.

Click Below for the Free Gift or Scan the QR Code with your phone

>>https://swiy.io/AsatruFreeBook<<

BONUS 3: FREE AUDIO VERSION OF THIS BOOK

If you love listening to audiobooks on-the-go or would enjoy a narration as you read along, I have great news for you. You can download the audiobook version of **Runes for Beginners** for FREE just by signing up for a FREE 30-day Audible trial!

VISIT THE FOLLOWING LINK:

https://swiy.io/RunesAudio

OR scan the QR code with your phone:

INTRODUCTION TO RUNES

There are runes for love, runes for protection, runes for healing, runes for desire, and runes that can be cast and interpreted to reveal the future. However, in order for a meaning to emerge, each rune must fall into its rightful place; so, you should never attempt to interpret them because they will not provide you with answers that actually concern you.

Runes have a huge amount of energy and can be employed in various ways. The runes have enormous power, but they are dormant until they are awakened by someone who understands them and knows how to harness them in divination or other sorts of magic. Although runes do not always provide obvious answers, their accuracy is astonishing when compared to lesser forms of occultism such as horoscopes or tarot cards.

The runes are an ancient system of divination that originated in Northern Europe. They are letters of the alphabet, but not like those we use today. The runes were carefully carved on stones called rune stones, and they were used to communicate with the Gods or Goddesses.

One could write their name on runes and cast them on the ground. From there, they would ask a question. They would read the runes that fell face up and interpret them as an answer to their question. The runes did not only serve divination purposes but were also used in magic spells, sometimes to summon the Gods or Goddesses. Even today, runes are important in divination and magic practices because they can help you discover things about yourself and your world.

Do runes really work? Over time, they might, but it all depends on your belief in them. If you believe runes are real, then they will affect your life over time and with enough practice. But that's not the only way runes can influence your life. If you recognize runes for what they are, letters of an alphabet that hold a particular meaning, then runes will help you learn and discover about the world around you in context to those runes.

This guide teaches readers how to read runes and explains their importance in divination can be applied to different aspects of life or even in a career.

In the following guide, you'll learn how runes were used in divination and magic, as well as their importance outside of that. You'll also be able to interpret runes on your own by learning the meanings of each rune and how they can be applied to elements of daily life, including love, work, wealth, and more!

Some runes have special meanings and qualities. Some runes seem more relevant to divination than others, but you are encouraged to find your meaning in each rune and enhance your runic journey through practice with runes.

Many people have found runes helpful throughout their daily lives, whether their careers, families, or spirit. For some, runes can be used as talismans to bring certain qualities in life and change the overall energy of a room, while for others, runes are part of daily routines and practices that have become habits for them.

It is worth noting here that runes are not meant to replace all aspects of daily life, but runes are an aid for when the individual feels they may help.

There is no right or wrong way to use runes in your life; runes have proven effective at changing the lives of many by providing insight into certain situations and guiding people on their paths. Now you can learn how to read and interpret your runes and use them for different purposes depending on what you need. Now it's time to go out and bring happiness into your life!

***

Runes are a set of symbols used for divination in Northern Europe. They communicate with spirits and divine the future. After many years, an interest in the runes resurfaced, and new adaptations were introduced.

Runes are one of the oldest known forms of writing, and their introduction dates back to before the introduction of Latin or Greek into the Nordic culture.

The introduction of Christianity did not mean that runes disappeared, although they were more commonly associated with paganism after this time. Runes remained in use throughout Northern Europe for hundreds of years after this time, often used by pagans because they were viewed as a form of magic and witchcraft.

Although early runes were carved into wood, especially elder wood that contained natural holes, they are most commonly carved onto stone or metal.

Runes were a means of magic for people who could not read or write, although this changed as literacy became more widespread.

In modern times runes have been reintroduced in different forms, such as decorative stones to be used in jewelry making or Scandinavian artwork with runic designs that can be found on clothing and bags.

Runes are seen as a form of art, and they can be interpreted in different ways by using symbols associated with them. The interpretation of the runes is made through divination.

Rune reading was often done by discerning the runes' message from knowledge found in ancient books on magic and witchcraft, where there were hundreds of interpretations for deciphering what the runes meant.

However, runes are used for more than just divination and magic. They also have magical qualities that can be used in rituals.

Some types of runes have evolved over centuries, and many modern adaptations no longer follow the old rules for carving or writing them down. Instead of using them to divine the future, many people today use runes as a way of focusing or grounding themselves and search online for different sets they can print out and keep in their pockets.

Runes are still used in divination today by runemasters and are often used by many people in daily life as a grounding tool.

These carvings are often simple, straight lines of a certain length and thickness, but they can also be very intricate.

Many people use runes for divination or grounding today. Although some rune masters use pendulums and crystals when casting these spells, many simpler methods exist for those who do not have any extras lying around.

Runes are carved onto certain objects, usually stones or metal; however, they can also be found on wooden sticks or paper. Runes were originally not written or read left to right but would instead be drawn vertically and read from the top down. This is still how they are used today for some people as a personal grounding tool.

Keep in touch with your intuition while you read and experiment with the knowledge contained inside, as this is the only way to effectively improve your skills in any form of magic. Have fun discovering and exploring the realm of the runes!

CHAPTER 1

UNCOVERING THE RUNES

Runes are ancient symbols that have been inscribed on all sorts of items throughout history. These runes, usually written in a left-to-right pattern and often carved into wood or stone, held magical significance for the Norse people who used them to write messages containing wisdom they believed could be obtained from the gods through these cryptic phrases. One particular rune looked like an arrow pointing upwards with three branches sprouting off it; this was called "Othila" by Odin himself when he whispered his secrets over a giant ash tree before giving birth to nine different kinds of runes appearing as sticks hung up within its trunk's hollow interior." Runes have a rich history and are still used in many magical practices such as divination and Norse mythology.

RUNES DEFINED

Runes are typically described as a magical alphabet used to write Germanic languages before introducing Latin alphabets. The definition of rune, however, does not end there. This can be the definition for an ordinary person who has little or no knowledge about history or in-depth information about something or someone else. But back to our definition: Runes are said to be runic alphabets that date back as far as several centuries Before the Common Era (BCE - the secular version of BC or before Christ). They were also commonly used during this time and even up until today in many countries, especially Europe.

When we look at modern-day stones that have been carved into different shapes with hard edges, we might be saying, "Those are runes!" In fact, that is not the definition of what genuine runes are. Genuine runes are made from wood or metal and have soft edges to signify an ancient definition in form and definition. They were usually used for writing purposes before paper was invented and markings on weapons and shields of warriors.

THE PROTO-GERMANIC AND NORSE ORIGIN OF THE WORD RUNE

The etymology of the word rune is disputed. Early common Germanic was like a linguistic patchwork, with sound changes happening in some words but not others. The dictionary-accepted rune is thought to have originated from the Norse word rún, which means 'mystery', and the Proto-Germanic word runo, which implies 'letter' or 'secret', and it likely comes from the Greek word "Ιούνιος" (Ioúnios), meaning 'ruler'.

 The rune in the words wōnjō, wōnskaga, and pynsą (wænsung) means 'vowel', but it may also stand for a short vowel or any vowel, like the penultimate modern English vowel (as in 'boys', 'ago'). The Old Norse word is cognate with English rune and German Rune.

There are many other theories about their etymology; some say they are from the root run- meaning 'secret' or 'whisper'. It should be noted that there is no hard definition of what a rune truly is, especially since its definition has been changed over time. However, one thing that runes will always have is an ancient definition in both definition and form.

NORSE MYTHOLOGY AND THE LEGEND OF THE RUNES

Norse mythology is rich in history, and the history of runes and Norse lore get intertwined. There are many theories on how the two have come together, but one thing that's for sure is that there is a connection between them.

Some scholars say that the Norse Vikings influenced the use of runes by people in other parts of Europe, such as Iceland. In addition, there is a theory that says that Christians created many false theories about the origin of runes and their uses to avoid being executed for practicing sorcery or paganism. This theory caused mixtures between European and Norse myths. It should be noted that even though these theories are different, this does not mean one theory is more accurate than the other, but rather that there is a connection in history between runes and Norse mythology.

Despite the fact that the runes were used throughout Europe by Germanic tribes, the only documented descriptions of their mythical origins that we have today are from the Nordic region. Because Christianization and the abolition of native beliefs took place a few centuries later in the northernmost areas of Europe than in the rest of Europe, the Scandinavians had more time than their southern counterparts to record their history and beliefs in writing.

The Poetic and Prose Eddas are two historical sources from which we can learn about Norse mythology. These works, which were transcribed in medieval times, contain famous songs and legends, such as the Hávamál, or "The Sayings of the High One," which is directly credited to Odin and from which we learn of the runes' origins. Elves, Dwarves, Giants, and gods like Odin, Thor, and Freya were depicted in these stories as marvelously complex and terrible beings and gods, providing great significance to the lives of these ancient people.

Odin is well-known for his shamanic and magical abilities, but they were taught to him by Freya. Odin was the Great Wanderer, renowned for his poetry, cunning in battle, and wisdom long before he embarked on his quest to discover the runes; once he did, they only enhanced his wondrous magic.

Perhaps the most appropriate place to begin a mythological examination of the runes is with Yggdrasil, the great tree. This tree, commonly identified as an ash tree and it is at the core of the Universe and in its roots and branches connects the nine worlds of Norse mythology. Everything is connected via Yggdrasil, which is frequently referred to as the "World Tree."

The Well of Urd—also known as the Well of Fate—is located at the bottom of Yggdrasill. It is a bottomless pool where the gods are said to convene every day. Norns—female beings from the world of the giants (referred to as jötnar)—are also present at this well. The Norns take care of Yggdrasill by safeguarding its roots and bathing it with sacred water from the Well of Urd.

The Norns are thought to weave the tapestry of fate into which all humans – and gods – are entangled. The Norns, more than any other being in Norse mythology, shape the path of major and little events by spinning, weaving, and severing fate's threads. They also carve runes into the trunk of Yggdrasil, in addition to their weaving. The runes' meanings, or intentions, are carried up the trunk and into the branches, affecting everything in the nine worlds that reside there, including Midgard, the world of humans.

It appears likely that runes were used for divination partly because of their association with the Norns, the fate weavers and legendary representations of time. However, the concepts of "fate" and "time" in Norse cosmology are not synonymous with how they are commonly defined in modern culture, which is critical to understand when working with the runes in divination.

Even though the Norns have always used runes, these magical symbols were not available to the gods—and thus to humans—until Odin found them through great self-sacrifice.

Odin intends to drink from Mimir's Well, also known as the "well of wisdom" or "fountain of wisdom" in the first narrative. As a result of sipping from the well every day, Mimir was a being who understood more about the universe than just about anyone. Mimir tells Odin that he can drink from the well but only if he gives up one of his eyes. Odin accomplishes this, becoming the "one-eyed deity" and earning a great deal of insight resulting from the sacrifice.

In the second narrative, Odin hears about the runes and seeks to learn more about them, so he travels to the Well of Urd, where the runes are kept. On the other hand, the runes are extremely powerful magical and information sources that do not disclose themselves to just anyone—not even gods. Odin realizes that he'll have to make another sacrifice if he wants the runes to respect him. This time, he uses his blade to pierce himself and hangs himself upside down from a branch of the huge tree Yggdrasil, which overlooks the Well of Urd. He remains there for nine days and nights, injured and upside down, refusing to let other gods offer him water, food, or any other type of help. Finally, in the water below, the runes—their shapes and secrets—are revealed to him.

The knowledge of the runes transforms Odin after enduring bodily agony, deprivation, and psychological loneliness (hanging from the tree for nine days and nights). In the poem Hávamál, Odin tells us that once he lifted the runes from the Well of Urd, he "grew and waxed in wisdom," discovering that he could now perform great feats of magic. He can utilize his new magical skills to assist himself and others in avoiding danger, vanquish adversaries, recover from injuries and illnesses, and even find love.

Odin may have been able to gain knowledge of the runes rather quickly (after his nine days and nights of self-sacrifice), but he was the god of wisdom. When it came to "ordinary mortals," it appears that some level of study and discipline and a specific talent for mystical activity were required. Those who sought out and effectively used this knowledge were known as "runemasters" in Norse culture, especially during the Viking era.

This is evident in the Eddic poem Rigsmál, which describes the origins of human society's "three classes" (serfs, free peasants, and nobles). There is a strong link between nobility and rune expertise in this area. Thrall, the first serf (or slave), Churl, the first free peasant, and Jarl (or "Earl"), the first nobleman, are all fathered by the deity Rig, also known as Heimdall.

Rig teaches the runes to Jarl once he is old enough to understand them. According to the poem, Jarl has several sons, but only the youngest of them, known as "Kon" or "King," understands the runes. This knowledge and the capacity to put it into practice through magical feats bring prestige upon Kon within his prominent family.

Runes are constantly mentioned in the epic, Saga of the Volsungs, and they play important roles in some of the stories. It narrates Sigurd, a mortal hero, "learning the runes" from Brunhilde, a Valkyrie. Sigurd had learned a little about the runes from his foster father, but Brunhilde knows even more and goes into great depth about the many types of runes, their magical uses, and how they should be carved depending on the occasion. She tells Sigurd, for example, to construct "wave runes" and burn them onto the oar to ensure safe travel at sea. There are various runes, each with its function, such as "victory runes," "speech runes," and "cure runes." Modern runemasters still follow these magical classifications. In another narrative from the Saga of the Volsungs, a note from Gudrun, a member of the royal family, was delivered to her brothers, warning them of impending treachery. Gudrun's message is intercepted, and the runes changed to make it appear as if she is inviting her brothers to visit. The message is examined by the wife of one of the brothers, who can see the original message beneath the change. She then cautions her husband not to leave home, "You must be very competent at interpreting runes if you think our sister has asked you to come."

In one of the most well-known stories from Egill's Saga, the hero, Egill, pays a visit to a woman who has been gravely ill and discovers whalebone with runes etched into it beside her bed in an attempt to heal her. However, whoever carved them was inept at rune magic and had made things worse for her. Egill, a Viking poet with a penchant for runes, carves the right symbols into a piece of antler and hides it under the woman's bed. She is almost instantly cured.

The runes are markings that symbolize letters of the alphabet as well as mystical signs. In fact, the runes were utilized for magical functions long before they were used for communication. The Prose and Poetic Eddas and several other sagas provide the mythology and lore surrounding the runes. We learn about the origins of the runes and the gods and creatures who brought them to us and showed us how to use them, such as Odin's sacrifice on the World Tree, through studying the lore and mythology of the ancient Norse people. The runes appear in many ancient Norse legends and myths, providing just enough insight and direction to begin our quest for discovery.

.

Chapter 2

Rune Evolution: A Journey Through Time

We'll travel through the evolution of the runes themselves from their very first iteration to their latest forms. Runes have long been employed in magic, for reasons such as cursing, blessing, and divination, as well as for communication. As the Norse and northern European cultures evolved, so did the runes. Runes have been with us from the dawn of time, from ancient tribal pagans to Viking traditions, and all the way through medieval and present times.

Runic History From Ancient to Modern Times

The earliest runes date from the 2nd century CE, and the latest date from around 1100. The most famous is probably the Tjängvide image stone (G 110), which covers both sides. It was found in a quarry near Torsåker in Sweden in 1640 and is now at the Swedish Museum of National Antiquities in Stockholm. The inscription commemorates an alleged Viking raid on England some 500 years earlier and details Norse paganism.

The finger-ring (OA.10262) was found in Carlisle, England. It is currently housed in the British Museum. The object is a gold finger-ring, engraved with a runic inscription around the hoop between nielloed lines; three letters continuing on inside of hoop. It contains 19 characters engraved on it that probably had religious or magical significance. Runes were most often carved on stone in this period, but some objects were cast in bronze. In 3000 BCE, runes seem to become less used and might have disappeared altogether had it not been for their use as ideograms or determinatives in casting lots, a practice recorded from around 100 CE.

An inscribed Anglo-Saxon cross shaft, known as the Ruthwell Cross, at Ruthwell Church near Whithorn, Scotland, contains three lines with Latin text and two battle-ax motifs below each of them. Above these is a shorter fourth line with three spear-like characters (likely ᛉᛈᛗᚠ). The inscription is still readable and states that King Oswald of Northumbria had the cross made in his family's memory.

There are also instances of the plural runas on coins from southern Sweden dating from around 300 CE. In addition, the term runor survived as a loan word in Middle English (runes) and was also current in Old Norse (runir). The Younger Futhark is the runes used by the 8th to 10th centuries.

The Anglo-Saxon Rune Poem (c. 1000 CE) says, "þæt wē ǣr [=wǣre] ūs æfenstaġn and laȝen œfenspræce and þā ȝēar ġē begǫrdon swā hit gēar to nīwan, oþðe hit ellenrōfte ond hit elne gēolod", i.e., "that we before were ash (áss) trees of the aefen-stæth (a type of pillars). And they gave us both names of honor after the manner of men, and for this reason, they called us [runes] first Othila, then Ehwaz". (Othila has also been translated as "one who accompanies" while Ehwāz translates to "horse"). The word "eihwaz," which did not survive into later runic usage, probably denoted a single-pole wooden yoke or strap.

The runes were encoded by using the Younger Futhark to encode modern texts based on ASCII or Unicode. This ended up producing letters that look exactly like Latin ("F" looking like "f," etc.) and can be easily typed onto computers today. Computers sort these letters based on how similar they are to modern Latin letters using the ASCII character encoding standard. This led to runes that look very similar (and in some cases identical) to those in inscriptions, but they are not actually rune-like, or anything close to Old Norse runes as most people imagine them today. It wasn't until around 936 CE, when Ólaf Tryggvason standardized the rules for writing with these symbols, that they became equivalent to modern Younger Futhark and thus only three "types" of runes: futhark, long-branch runes, and short-twig runes. The short branch was used for "ū" while the long branch was used for the other vowels. At least six runic rowels were designed specifically for one use, while additional variants were created for specific types of magic. The three "types" are actually futhorc runes (they looked like Latin) which the Younger Futhark encoded.

The Codex Regius (ca. 1260) is a medieval Icelandic manuscript that contains an extensive list of runes spanning sixteen pages.

Germanic tribes used their swords to remove wood shavings from fences and then wrote on those with charred sticks (or possibly burnt wood). The Gaulish Celts marked trees using sword strokes. Celtic druids would inscribe on oak wands or scapulae inscriptions significant to their practices, such as "Meadō" meaning "with respect to divination" and a common inscription at sites of religious ceremonies, though probably interpreted incorrectly as "méadús" (victory). In any case, Galasso (1982) notes that in the 1st century BCE, Cicero already complained about Gaulish warriors writing secret messages on trees ("silentiarios Gallos indeclinabili ligno notatos"). It is possible that this source used the Latin word 'runa' for something else than the Old Norse meaning 'secret writing', but since "méadús" is not a Latin word, the inscription cannot be translated as such.

The oldest one ever found dates back to 1040 CE, and it was discovered in Norway's Sølsnes. Researchers couldn't really tell what Anglo-Saxon runes meant until they started comparing them with medieval copies of the alphabet. The reason for this is that nobody really knew how to read or write in runes before then. The oldest runic inscriptions are from around 200 CE, and the last ones were written in 1205 CE.

The runes' alphabetical order is also called futhark. The Vikings devised it based on known letters until the 6th century CE (theory says they have replaced all of them with fule runes). They had a single rune for each letter and added some additional characters to make it easier to write words. The Elder Futhark consisted of 24 runes, while the rest have been added later.

The number of runes was originally 24, later expanded to 29, then up to 50. The order is based on the Aryan numerals with different characters representing each value: 1 to 10, 20, 30, 40 and 100.

Runes have undergone changes in meaning and representation from the 150 runes attested to during the Viking Age. In early medieval times, runes were used for writing on stone or wood, but they found other uses as recorded by runic texts such as inscriptional runes.

An extensive study into runic magic was written by Johannes Bureus entitled "Runa" from 1555 AD. Bureus gives one of the first "modern" interpretations of runes, and he describes the multiple ways runes were used in combination with each other.

Linguistic studies of runes were common during the 17th century. In 1665, Johan Runge published a Latin treatise on runes called "Runein", which focused more on how runes related to phonetics rather than magic or divination as earlier runic works did. Jens Worsaae also studied runes at this time period, but his work was unknown until it was translated into English in 1832 by James C. Horne. He suggested that runes had been imported from Northern Europe to Denmark after the Younger Futhark appeared there (ca 800 CE). This theory is contradicted by how widespread runes were found throughout Scandinavia and most of England.

The runes survived into the 18th century when runes were still used for birthstones in Sweden. The Swedish government abolished the use of runes because they were seen as a sign of witchcraft and magic. They had become popular during the Enlightenment Age (1700s) due to witch-hunting laws. Finally, today, runes have been revived in modern practices such as witchcraft or Neo-Paganism but primarily through divination than actual inscription of objects with runes.

With the introduction of runes into Nazi ideology, runes became linked with Nordicism and Aryanism. Although archeologists and linguists had discovered runes, there was little interest in runes for a long period of time until they were necessary as part of the Nazi agenda. In more modern times, runes are no longer associated with politics but rather as one's personal identity based on aesthetics and philosophy.

Today runes are no longer considered a sign of nationalism, but instead, one's personal identity based on aesthetics and philosophy can be joined with politics. Runes are generally promoted by Neopagans (usually Wiccans), who see them as symbols of magic or spirituality, showing how far from the original meaning runes have come today. Although still linked to modern political groups, Neo-paganism promotes runes for aesthetic reasons.

THE DIFFERENT RUNIC ALPHABETS

The runes were composed of strokes, which were either vertical or slanted. They could even be diagonal, as seen in runes write; since runes represented both consonant sounds and vowel sounds, runes had to be simple enough so that they would not become confused with another rune. Towards the end of their use, runes began to appear more angular with sharp edges. The runes in use during that period are called the Futharkh (red runes) because there is a certain amount of red appearing in them.

The Elderfuthark was developed by adding one more row of runes above the original three rows. It consisted of 24 runes. Each rune has a name and a meaning, making it easy to use runes for magic and divination.

The Anglo-Saxon runes were similar to the Elderfuthark runes but with less complicated names and meanings. Anglo-Saxon runes had no lowercase letters because the runes did not need a change to adapt to parchment.

The runes used during the Viking age were called Younger Futhark runes, and they consisted of 16 runes. They first appeared in Scandinavia, but because runes could be easily transported with the Vikings who traveled around their conquered territories, runes started to appear in different countries as other nations adopted runes.

The Scandinavian runes evolved from the Elder Futhark runes, they also consisted of 24 runes, and each rune had a name and a meaning. After the Viking conquest of England in 1066, the Anglo-Saxon runes gradually fell into disuse. This was mainly because most runic inscriptions found after that date are in Scandinavian runes.

The Futhark runes are divided into three groups of eight runes each, known as ætt. The runes in each group all have a name, and the rune names within an ætt seem to be related.

Runes were usually carved on stones, wood or metal. In other cases, runes were painted on with dye or ink. Runes could also be written on parchment, but there was no lowercase lettering. The runes were read from left to right and downwards, just like the modern Latin alphabet.

Even though runes were developed before the Latin alphabet, runes lost popularity until they suddenly became fashionable again during the Renaissance period.

Runes can be written with any pencil, pen, or chalk, and when they are scratched onto wood using a nail or awl, the runes are called runes cut. Runes incised are runes carved into stone or similar material using a chisel style cutting tool, and runes hammered are made by applying force to a chisel so that it cuts deep lines into the stone's surface.

DEVELOPMENT OF THE PRESENT RUNIC ALPHABET

Runes were used in many ancient cultures to express spiritual concepts and were written as symbols rather than letters. Essentially, runes are a form of writing used for various purposes such as communication and magic rituals. Out of all languages that have used runes, they are most commonly associated with ancient Germanic languages, most commonly the Norse and Anglo-Saxon languages. Many cultures created different types of runes for writing; many were monolithic, while others had two parallel lines.

Runes have been used in various ways throughout human history. Some examples include written communication, magical rituals, divination, and as part of artwork. One way runes were used as a form of communication is through the fact that rune stones were carved and left behind for future generations to read. Many rune stones exist today containing information about the person who created them, such as their name or title. Runes were also frequently used in magic rituals. One notable example is the Icelandic Rune Poem, which was used in various spells and magic rituals. Another way in which runes were used is as part of artwork. Carvings of runic symbols have been found on various objects such as brooches, jewelry, and even weapons like spears and swords.

Runes have been used for many different purposes throughout the centuries, from commemorating the name and title of a historical figure for future generations to conveying messages about love, luck, and prosperity. Whether they are being used as tools for communication or magic rituals, it is clear that humans have been fascinated by runes for thousands of years.

Out of all languages that have used runes, they are most commonly associated with ancient Germanic languages, most commonly the Norse and Anglo-Saxon languages. Many cultures created different types of runes for writing, either monolithic or two parallel lines.

The symbol of a rune is an ancient letter that contains magical significance. The word "rune" comes from the old Norse word rún, which means secret or mystery. A rune is any letter carved into stone or wood and then left for future generations to read. Runes were used in the ancient world by various cultures, including the Germanic, Norse and Anglo-Saxon peoples. Runes were used for many purposes, including writing that allowed people to communicate secret messages. The earliest runes were monolithic; they had no parallel lines and could be carved on anything such as wood or metal. As time went on, people realized that a system needed to be created to learn the symbols and their meanings, so parallel lines were created. The ancient Greeks believed that runes allowed you to gain knowledge, wisdom, and power by carving them on stones. They used them as a tool to create amulets and talismans, which they believed could protect them from evil or bring good fortune. It is interesting that in many cultures, the same symbols are used for very different things. For instance, an X-shaped arrow is a rune that symbolizes power and strength to some cultures, but it signifies death and evil in Norse culture.

In Runic alphabets such as Elder Futhark (2nd to 8th centuries AD), the Haglaz rune ᚺ was used to write Proto-Norse, or Old Norse when it first appeared in the mid-2nd century. In later Scandinavian runes, the Elder Futhark ᚺ was reduced to the simple X-shape, which is now known as Icelandic graph 'Z'. The Anglo-Saxon futhorc (4th to 9th centuries AD) continued the Elder Futhark tradition and added four runes to the Younger Futhark: thorn Þ, wynn ᚹ, ȝ (yogh) ᚸ and geolu g. Wynn is an archaic letter appearing on the golden bracteate found in Schleswig and is a variant of ᚹ. The Younger Futhark (8th-11th centuries) introduced the Hagalaz rune ᚦ. The addition of the "yogh" letter required two new runes since there were now three (ᚠ ᚷ ᚻ). These inventions are attributed to the Danish king, Harald Bluetooth Gormsson. The rune hagall (Hagalaz) is named in his honor. In the modern Norwegian Rune Poem, the name of all 16 runes begins with hagall (ᚺᛁᚴᛒᚠ), which means "whale."

Runic inscriptions were found throughout the Roman Empire on stone monuments and objects such as jewelry, weapons, and tools. However, only a few runic inscriptions have been found in Britain (the largest collection is over 100 stones at Ruthwell Cross). Most of the rune stones found in England are from Scandinavia. We find a wide variety of images on these rune stones, including horses and riders, ships and boats, dragons and snakes, warriors and sea monsters, deities, humans, birds, insects, and plants. One particularly intriguing puzzle was the spearhead found in 1848 at Pierrepont Hall near Kingston upon Hull. It had a runic inscription carved on it and was dated to the 9th century; however, no one could translate it until 1928 when H. R. Loyn found that the inscription spelled the words "Here lies Halfdan, I beg you for God's sake, give my lord my bones." The spearhead probably came from Scandinavia but is an interesting example of how runes were used far away from their homeland.

From Viking Age graves in England and elsewhere, we have only a few examples of Runic inscriptions on jewelry or weapons— generally consisting of names or brief messages translated to "Ali's hilt," inscribed on Ali the Bold's sword and inlaid with silver. The use of runic scripts declined as time passed, though it is still found in everyday life.

The end of the Viking Age saw the decline of the Norse written language. The people still spoke Old Norse but began to have difficulty understanding texts composed earlier than their lifetime. To preserve these earlier writings, scribes began spelling words phonetically and writing in the alphabet known as "Medieval runes" or "the first language" (runic characters are called futhork). This process is referred to as Latinization, and despite the change of script, no changes were made for morphology. The language began to be influenced by Old Norse, a dialect of Old West Norse—these two dialects differed only slightly, but both evolved into modern-day Icelandic and Norwegian. Today Icelandic is written using Latin letters; however, it still retains some features distinguishing it from other languages such as English. For example, unlike most Germanic languages that use 'th' for /θ/ (e.g., thing vs. than), Icelandic uses 'þ' ('thorn') instead, and unlike English, it also uses 'ð' ('eth'). Also, Icelandic does not use the letters J or U (uppercase) but instead uses the same letter for both /j/ and /w/.

The Younger Futhark or simply futhark refers to a period from the 8th century through the 11th century when Scandinavians adopted and further developed the Germanic Runic Script for their use, adding 16 new characters to bring it up to a total of 24 runes. The order of these 16 or 24 Elder Runes is based on shape (ᛊᛒᚱ → ᚷᛏ → ᚺ). But since they were added at different times, they do not have a fixed order.

CHAPTER 3

RUNIC ORIGINS AND PAGANISM

While runologists argue over many of the details of the historical origins of runic writing, there is widespread agreement on a general outline. The runes are presumed to have been derived from one of the many Old Italic alphabets in use among the Mediterranean peoples of the first century CE, who lived to the south of the Germanic tribes. The oldest known example of a Germanic language rune is the Elder Futhark inscription on the Golden Horns of Gallehus, which are dated back to 401-449 CE. Viking Age inscriptions are found on all Scandinavian monuments from that period onwards and remain visible as long as the weathering has not been too severe.

The runes themselves were developed in the first century CE, during the early years of Roman occupation, most likely by Germanic peoples living southeast of Scandinavia. It is assumed that these runes were used for simple messages (mostly numbers and personal names), similar to how we might use initials or abbreviations today. Runestones with more elaborate messages appeared soon after. Some runestones contain lengthy texts, most famously the Viking Age inscription on the Ruthwell Cross.

Runic inscriptions are found across all parts of Scandinavia, from Norway in the west to Sweden and Iceland in the east and as far south as Denmark. They also appear outside Scandinavia on artifacts such as weapons and jewelry discovered as far away as England, Ireland and Romania.

Today, there are more than 1,100 known inscriptions in the Elder Futhark script from Bornholm to Trondheim. They have been discovered on every object imaginable: weapons, tools, jewelry, wooden tablets and stone monuments (including runestones). All but thirty of these inscriptions have been found in Scandinavia.

The oldest known examples are from Överhogdal and date to the late fourth century CE, slightly earlier than those on the Gallehus horns. The younger futhark develops out of the older one over time, showing a genuinely living script. While some runestones are treated as art objects by museums and collectors, most of them are still standing where they were erected centuries ago.

But what does the word 'runic' mean? The term 'rune' is derived from an Old Norse word meaning both letters and secret or mystery, while the suffix -ic comes directly from Latin (as in historic, mechanic, aesthetic and so on). It is widely accepted that the word was borrowed into Old English as runic, but what does it mean?

In Old English usage, the term 'run' covers several related ideas. There is a noun 'rune', meaning secret or mystery (used in this way in Beowulf), and a verb 'runean', meaning to whisper or mumble (as in the line from The Battle of Maldon: 'This Byrhtnoth boded, / With his last breath he branded / The rune upon the thanes'). There are also many compounds with 'rune' as their second element, such as 'be-rune', 'for-rune', 'on-rune' and the like.

Where do these words come from? It is widely assumed that they are based on the earlier word 'runa' found in Old Norse texts, which also means secret or mystery. Can we find any clues as to how this meaning developed? There is a fascinating passage in the Old English translation of Bede's Ecclesiastical History of the English People (composed by the Northumbrian monk Alfred c. 890 CE) where he describes how Christianity was brought to England:

'They [the pagans] made replies neither openly nor secretly, but with crafty cunning they hoped to elude him [the missionary]. So it was that not openly, nor in words, but in crafty cunning or by rune-craft, as I may call it, they worshiped their idols.'

The term 'rune-craft' here is parallel with Old English words such as galdorcræft and galdricge (meaning spells, charms and magic incantations). The word 'rune' in this sense is also used by the Old English translation of the biblical Book of Proverbs. In the chapter on wisdom, for example, we read:

'But if thou wilt be wise as serpents, and harmless as doves, thou shalt be able to endure all things, and nothing shall overcome thee.'

The phrase 'overcome' here is rendered as 'onrune' (i.e., overcome by the runes). But how do we explain the suggestion that rune-craft was a cunning or crafty activity? Could this be derived from runa in Old Norse, which means both secret and cunning?

The word 'rune' itself also has a fascinating pedigree. Some scholars have suggested it may be related to the Latin verb 'monere' or 'munire', meaning to warn or advise. There is a noun 'rūnōs' that appears in Old Irish sources as 'rúan' (plural rúananna), meaning magic or incantation. If this is related to the Latin monere, it would appear possible that early Germanic speakers borrowed this word from their Celtic neighbors and then redefined its meaning as secret or mystery over time.

The word 'rune' means 'secret or mystery' in Old English, but a more literal meaning of the word is 'mystery letter'. The letters themselves became associated with magic and sorcery from early on in their use. Over time, this sense of mystery was transferred to the letters themselves: they represented hidden knowledge, which could be revealed only through proper study and learning. By the 11th century CE, this   was   a widespread belief in medieval Europe, and it is reflected in the following Latin epitaph for a knight called Baudricus:

'The more he was given to reading and the learning of letters, the more did he become devoted to God. He had read much, but still believed more.'

We can see how deeply this idea was ingrained in the culture of the time. It is also significant that Baudricus was praised for his belief rather than his skill in combat; reading and learning at this time were much more highly valued than physical prowess or martial skill.

PAGAN CONTEXT

In pagan Germanic society, runes had a high status as magical signs associated with Odin, the highest god in their pantheon. They were also closely associated with other gods and goddesses of war and death, such as Týr (or Tiw in old english), Tyrfing, Óðinn, Vé and others, depicted on several runestones from Scandinavia. The word 'rune' did not have a single meaning for the pagan Scandinavians; rather, it was a vast array of signifiers denoting concepts such as magic, war, wealth and social status.

For   example,   the   runic   inscription   on   the "Västra Strö 2 Runestone" (DR 335) from Denmark reads:

Faðir had this stone cut (by Tiw) in memory of Bjôrn, who owned a ship with him.'

The term 'rune of victory' is what we would today call the name Tyrfing. This shows how closely associated runes were with their owners and concepts; they were a form of identity and ownership.

Runic inscriptions appear in Scandinavia from around 4th-5th century onwards, but the alphabet is much older than this. It likely originated in the 2nd century CE and was used mainly for writing on wood, alongside the Latin alphabet. It is thought that runes were probably first introduced to Scandinavia from Germanic areas further south as a writing system. Still, over time they developed their significance within Scandinavian pagan society.

ODIN AND THE RUNES

In Old Norse sources, Odin is said to have sacrificed one of his eyes to obtain wisdom. He also hung himself on a great tree for nine days and nights - the Yggdrasil - to achieve higher levels of awareness; during this time, he received knowledge from the runes and their secret gifts. The word 'runa' is from the same Proto-Germanic root as 'raven', because these birds were apparently used in divination rituals to reveal secret knowledge.

The most well-known account of this in Old Norse literature is found in Grímnismál, a part of the Poetic Edda:

'High on the tree Odin Power bore me,

Surge of wisdom I received from Wotan;

All the Runes he gave to me.

Then first I knew what power they held.'

The woodpecker was associated with runes because it uses its beak to peck into trees to search for insects. Its ability to find hidden sources of nourishment was compared with how runes revealed things that were difficult to find. Odin's sacrifice of an eye is similar: he peered down into the well at Mímir's spring and sacrificed his right eye so that it would not dry up like all the other parts of Yggdrasil. He hung himself from the branches of Yggdrasil to gain knowledge to benefit mankind and understand how the world worked. Odin was associated with many different aspects of life, but his relationships with wisdom and runes were vital to his role as a god. This is why he is known as 'the wise one who knows everything' - in the Prose Edda he explains to Gangleri, one of his human visitors:

'I know all things that are yet to come and many things which have gone by - but most people make their own guesses.'

Being associated with magic, they gave people power over that which they could not control. Some of Odin's wisdom had been given to him by the runes, but his other knowledge he gained through self-sacrifice and realizing who it was that needed to gain wisdom.

RUNES AS MAGICAL SIGNS

The Anglo-Saxons used the letters of their own alphabet for writing but also employed Germanic runes in a way similar to that of the Scandinavians. It was believed that runes were imbued with magical power and they could be used to summon the dead, predict a person's future or provide protection for their owner. There are many surviving Anglo-Saxon charms that refer to runes as magic signs, including one found on a 10th-century CE bone in England which reads:

'What manner of man have I? He has (the) runes of ægir. What type have I? It is a runic one.'

Having knowledge of runes enabled Odin to look into the future and see what would happen; this is called 'being wise in the ways of wisdom' (Fjölsvinnsmál). This is why he was known as 'the one-eyed man who knows many things'.

The runes can also be thought of as being used to protect a person, their family or property. For example, using runes for magical protection is found in Hávamál where Odin says:

'Runes shall be able to help you if they are carved on wood; a knowledgeable man knows this.'

The runes are known as Anglo-Saxon futhorc and include alphabets and special characters, which were used for magical purposes.

Odin went on to explain:

'I know a twelfth one if I see, carved on wood; cut on the bark of a tree, if you carve them in a row. Know well how to carve them: carved on an arrow or on the shaft of a spear, so that it gets victory; graven on a sword hilt, so that no sword fails.'

Runes also had their place in magical practices which were used for divination. One of the great rune poems says:

'Runic letters, carved on wood, you must believe what you carve.'

These runes were used to make predictions about a person or event in the future by being able to see what would happen. Even though it is possible that the Vikings could have made these types of predictions using their skills and knowledge, it is important to remember that they were also a superstitious lot. The runes did give them an added power.

Runes as Letters of Magic

There are many instances where Anglo-Saxon charms refer to rune staves or futharks to cast spells. For example, this one from England refers to a rune stave:

'If you carve these using runes on a horse's eye, which can see very well at night, then the man who carved it will take away all that he looks at.'

This Anglo-Saxon charm has instructions about what to do with the rune so that magic will be attempted. It also shows that the Anglo-Saxons magically used runes with the horse's eyes to create a sense of awe and wonder, which is very similar to how the Norsemen thought about them. Other charms show that they also believed it was possible to use runes for chanting spells or even hanging them around a person's neck:

'Runic writings, which you have written on a piece of linen cloth, and hung around the neck of a boy who has not yet become a man.'

The writer believed that this rune should be taken off the boy's neck before he became a man as it would cause him to have spells. This shows that magic was linked with runes from an early date and that the Anglo-Saxons were not so different from the Norsemen who also believed in it.

The runic inscription was one of the most important types of magic for both Anglo-Saxons and Vikings. It was not only used to cast spells but also to determine when something would happen; this is known as divination. It was a commonly accepted practice and enabled people to control what would happen around them.

CHAPTER 4

RUNES AND DIVINATION: THE TRUTH
REVEALED

The account of Odin's acquisition of the runes is told in Norse mythology. It's a story of sacrifice, of Odin, spending nine days and nine nights speared in the side on the World Tree before bringing the runes from the Well of Wyrd. In its way, taking the runes from the well at the base of Yggdrasil was divination in the sense that he was looking for answers and information. Odin would gain immense knowledge as he brought the runes forth, and each rune represented that knowledge. This narrative, along with numerous other references in the Poetic Edda, demonstrates what we know about runic divination.

We will learn about the history of runes and divination, how to use runes for divination, and how to make your own set of runestones. The steps to take to establish a relationship with the runes involving your own intuitive experience will also be discussed.

WHAT IS RUNIC DIVINATION?

Divination is the art of foretelling or predicting future events. This can be done with various methods, such as rune stones, slips of paper, or the use of tarot cards. The Futhark runes are best utilized in divination. The Germanic-inspired runes were used to cast lots and to divine the future. Divination has been around for centuries. It can be traced back to the ancients who extensively studied documented techniques that would enable them to predict what was going on in their futures or take stock of their present state.

HOW ARE RUNES USED IN DIVINATION?

Runes share a deep and ancient history with divination, which has been used to understand the future and our place in the Universe. Runes are thought to be a set of symbols that have power in themselves. The Elder Futhark runes created them, but now there are many more than just those. The word "rune" is derived from an Old Norse word meaning "secret knowledge" or "mystery." To use runes for divination, we must find out what they do, what they represent, and how they can be used. The best way is if we sit down and meditate on them. When working with runes for divination, we need to remember that each rune has its mysteries and messages.

One message might be very different from another. Sometimes when we draw runes for divination, the runes might not speak to us directly, but they are still there for a reason. Sometimes runes can be markings on paper. They don't have their meaning unless you give it to them. The runes are powerful because of what we believe them to mean.

Many runes represent all kinds of energies (the 'elements'), astrological planets, colors, directions (North East South West), or glyphs for other objects like pentagrams. After meditating and learning about runes, you will gain your resonance and meanings from them. Some of them take time to show their power, while others work instantly because, unlike runes used for divination, runes for spellcraft are to be immediately put into action.

One of the most common uses runes have in divination is casting runes, which has been utilized to foresee future events. In this method, runes are cast on the ground or somewhere else. They reveal their messages through patterns they leave behind or by lying directly on top of each other with opposite meanings (opposites attract). Each rune offers its unique message when cast, although there is no correct way to draw them. By doing this, we might find questions that need answering pop up from nowhere. Taking time out each day can help us tune into our intuition and enhance our chakras; both are useful in divining with runes.

One must have a clear mind when using runes for divination or casting runes because if the mind is too busy, it will block out all other messages the runes may be trying to give you. We absorb information in runes through our intuition which means clearing your mind before drawing runes for divination. Try not to think of anything else but the runes as they are being drawn and look over them at least three times and then try meditating on them after that. It's best that one doesn't rush but takes their time to draw each rune slowly yet steadily.

Another common practice for divination is through runestones, consisting of runes carved onto or painted on small rocks or other small pieces of stone. Runestones give off a feeling when you hold them in your hand while casting the runes, helping everyone's energies merge with the runes and that person's intention to meditate on their meaning. The best way for most people to start is by creating runestones yourself at home, taking time with each rune carving so that they can absorb your energy into themselves; once this process has happened, you will know it because all of your runes will feel right for themselves individually to select from every time you draw them out while doing divination.

When runes are drawn from runestones, they can either be placed outside of our body on the ground or can be cast onto the inside of a circle. If you wish to use runes for divination in this manner, get a new deck that contains runestones, not tarot cards; runes and runestones have much more power than tarot cards do, so your messages will come out stronger. Tarots ask open-ended questions about life while runes directly answer them. Start simple by asking what is going on in your love life: How will it go tomorrow? Will I see my crush again soon? What should I wear today? You'll find answers very quickly if you focus hard enough to tune into their energies coming through into your own. The runes will communicate with you through your intuition, just like runestones do.

You can also use runes for divination by applying runes on the body so that they cover up certain areas of the body, so only one rune is revealed at each part of the body drawn on (i.e., shoulder=fehu, head=uruz). Cover all of your runes except for one or two runes altogether to ask yes or no questions and get answers from them. Once this has been mastered, you will understand what runes are telling you immediately without having to look them up in a book because that is how powerful you have become with using runes.

With runes, divination has been used as a way for finding answers to questions we might have while we're meditating or studying runes, using runestones and runes are great ways of getting started into both divination and spellcraft with runes on the side because there is no right way to cast runes or use runes stones so you will feel these energies coming through into your intuition (everyone's intuition works differently).

Runes and divination may seem complicated, but once you get started into runes with runes, divination becomes a natural thing. And remember that runes are not limited to just runestones.

How to make runes:

There are many ways to make runes. A simple way is to take a piece of wood and carve runes into it. It has been said that runes can be made from anything with four corners, like a book or a cup.

A rune set must be made from materials you feel have magical powers or properties so that when runes are handled, their powers may be transmitted to the person using them.

Runes may be bought readymade, but unless runes come from a source that you trust to have consisted of magically potent materials, it is best if you cast runes yourself for divination or magic. Runes may be made from natural materials, such as wood, stone, metal, clay, etc.

You can find runes in many different places. If runes are bought readymade, and you later wish to cast runes for divination so that they can reveal something about your future, then go through the procedures which I have already described using runes that you bought readymade.

How to establish a relationship with your runes:

Runes must become ingrained in an individual's consciousness through personal experience and meditation, as only then can runes be correctly handled and divination performed and interpreted.

Before you employ the runes for divination, get to know them. On paper, write about runes; in books, read about runes.

However, this does not make you one with the runes; they must also become one with you. Your knowledge of runes will be useless if the runes cannot provide insight into life's challenges. The ideal method to become one with runes is to meditate on them often enough that their patterns become as recognizable to you as the runes on a page. Before you do any divination, make sure you follow this step.

CASTING RUNES FOR DIVINATION

You cannot become a rune genius simply by possessing the runes; you must put runes in their places before they can produce results, no matter how much you study and master them. The runes have great powers that must be awakened, and this can only be done through the arduous route of human experience.

Divining should be done in a peaceful and tranquil environment. As a result, runes should only be used when you are alone.

Before casting the runes, focus on them because they each hold their source of inspiration; then use them to decipher the runes patterns or pictures that arise during divination. Pay no attention to rune-related coincidences; always remember that such events are frequently the result of chance or coincidence.

It is vital to first reflect on the circumstance that you are concerned about. Then, before casting runes for a response, ask yourself some questions about the situation. This connects your subconscious mind to the universal unconscious mind, allowing you to seek assistance from higher levels. Because runes do not respond to direct questions during divination, it is necessary to pose a question in your head before casting the runes.

When using runes for divination, hold them lightly between the thumb and fingers of your right hand, forming a cross or an X as you hold them. This will assist you in avoiding making unintentional movements that could cause runes to fall out of your hand during casting.

When runes are thrown on a table or other surface, they should be read from left to right, as most Asian people do; however, runes cast for love or marriage must be read clockwise. Because runes are only thrown for love or marriage when a clockwise circulation of energy occurs, this means that runes should be interpreted in the same direction as they are cast.

The surface on which runes are put for casting should be clean, smooth, and free of any imperfections; white fabric is the best choice. If runes are to be cast on cloth, they should be set out no more than two runes apart to allow the runes to lie close together and to prevent the runes from being read.

It's crucial to establish a relationship with the runes based on personal experience because the best way to get results in divination is to perform it regularly, just like everything else. You can add meanings to legends that are personal to your own life to enhance the usual mythological readings.

Even if the scenario does not appear to be critical, cast runes repeatedly every day so that the runes acquire familiarity with your numerous situations. The runes will gain their strength and reveal answers via automatic writing.

If you want to know about anything that will happen in the next three days, you should cast runes on Monday evening so that they are ready to interpret on Wednesday morning. All runes should lie in stillness overnight whenever possible, but this is not always possible.

When using runes for divination, it's crucial to lay them out at the same time each day. This helps the runes to grow comfortable with your specific problem, allowing them to assist you better.

It's vital to remember this while utilizing runes for divination: the runes are never wrong; it's the interpreter who would be. You may have expected someone to enter your life who never did, or you may have passed up an opportunity to make money by selling something and kept it instead. If runes were cast and interpreted to suggest that selling the object would have brought you money, you could blame yourself for not selling it when runes showed your error.

HOW TO PROTECT YOUR RUNES FROM OTHERS WHO MIGHT TRY TO DISRUPT THEIR ENERGIES

The runes possess certain peculiarities which might almost be termed supernatural. In the hands of one who understands them, they certainly possess power and insight that makes them, to some extent, a divining force. For this reason, runes should not be exposed to anyone without the key who may attempt to misuse them. To do so would be like putting dynamite in untrained hands, for runes, once used in divination, are active forces, both good and bad, and can produce striking results when foolishly handled or wrongly directed. They should never be placed upon an altar or other place where they can fall into the wrong hands or about the neck of any person except by one initiated into runes.

The runes are particularly fitted for divination. They possess a directness and incisiveness, which makes them singularly effective. When the runes are employed in this way, they become active agents and produce striking results when properly used under careful and competent direction. They should never be exposed to anyone except the one to whom they have been given, nor should they ever be cast carelessly upon an altar or place where they can fall into untrained hands, as their effect is deadly when misdirected by those not in sympathy with them. To do so would be like putting dynamite in the hands of children; it would bring about disaster even if rightly directed, while if wrongly directed, might annihilate anyone who came within their range.

There is no doubt that runes make excellent divination tools because they were originally made for this purpose in mind. Runes have been used to predict the future since their creation, whether through formalized methods or simply tossing them around a fire on an evening with friends and family when issues arose among people. They are especially useful in divining the future because they were created as a direct representation of the runes themselves. The runes contribute their energy and wisdom to our readings, which helps us receive more accurate results than if done with runes that haven't been developed into a relationship.

The runes are particularly suited to divination, and in the hands of one who understands them, they certainly possess certain peculiarities which might almost be termed supernatural.

CHAPTER 5

THE POWER OF RUNE MAGIC

The runes are a system used to record words and stories, but they have many more uses. We understand runic power because we see it in Norse lore and objects found from archeological digs. By understanding how these forces work with our goals for this world and beyond, we can use them wisely to call on help when needed most!

The discovery of the runes has fascinated many for centuries. In Norse mythology, Odin was said to have found them and used them as a means to predict fate. The Poetic Edda tells us more about their history and use. It also states that the runes are gifts from Odin, and he gave them to the humans as a means of teaching. They were used to ensure justice during disputes between chieftains. Rune magic has been around for centuries in Norse culture across Northern Europe.

Odin was the Norse god of wisdom, battle, and poetry. His name is also associated with being a shapeshifter which may have contributed to his discovery that runes are powerful symbols capable of communicating messages from otherworldly beings like Norns and mighty deities. Runestones are found near burial sites and locations of mystical importance, which tells us that the stone serves as an artifact to commemorate the dead or an attempt at scrying on behalf of those who would do it for divination purposes.

The towering Björketorp Runestone stands 14 feet tall and is one of the most well-known runestones. It creates a circle with two other enormous stones, but on top lies an Elder Futhark warning engraved in elegant runes that are several inches deep with small rocks piled at its base for decoration. The inscription in the Elder Futhark says, "I, master of the runes, conceal here runes of power. Incessantly [plagued by] maleficence, [doomed to] insidious death [is] he who breaks this [monument]."

WHAT IS RUNE MAGIC?

Runes come in all shapes and sizes, but they are used to write a variety of languages. To perform magic using runes, you can either use rune scripts that make an equation following sequential order similar to how letters build words; bind runes where we mix the rune styles for focused intent and success talismans to bring good fortune. Rune magic is an ancient form of magical practice and has been used to create amulets and talismans, and the language itself has been linked to the early Norse alphabet. Rune magic has also evolved.

Many famous Rune Masters of the time, including Helgi, Harbard, and Wulff, could create binding runes to bind or banish creatures from their lands. Rune magic has been used more in the past than today, but that does not mean it is any less powerful.

This knowledge tells us that runes have deep ties to the Scandinavian culture and history, and they have become one of its oldest symbols. Rune magic can be used for good or evil, as it has been throughout Norse history. It can be used to help crops grow or even kill another human in a duel. Rune powers always have consequences, but it is up to the magician to decide whether or not they are right for their cause.

Rune magic has been used for centuries, and generations have passed down this knowledge from teacher to student. Rune energies can be used for spells that are meant to draw luck, and they can also be used in various ways, such as casting off bad luck or protecting what you value from evil spirits or intrusive thoughts. There is an endless list of possibilities with the runes if one chooses to cultivate them, and Rune magic is still practiced today. Rune magic can be used for both good and evil; the choice is yours.

Runes are symbols based on their meaning with the intention of the desired outcome or result in mind. Rune meanings vary from region to region and person to person. Rune energies are just as powerful as other ancient forms of magical practice like astrology, numerology, and tarot.

HOW TO USE RUNES IN MODERN MAGIC:

First, the Norse runemasters would be unconcerned about what Wiccans and other Neopagans could call "dark" or "negative" magic. In many situations, rune spells for influencing people and delivering harm to foes were plentiful and deemed vital. We, on the other hand, advocate for the modern magical ethic of "hurt none."

Second, is it possible that employing the incorrect runes by accident will have bad or otherwise unforeseen consequences? Any magic might have unintended results, which is why it's always a good idea to think about how you'll convey your wishes to the Universe. Using the "wrong" runes, on the other hand, is more likely to render your magic unsuccessful rather than damaging. The quality of your focused intention during the work is what matters most. To activate the powers of any rune, you must have your energy present, just like with any other magical item.

When using runes in modern magic, you can purchase them from a variety of sources. You can buy your runes in bulk and have them shipped to you, or you can go to a store that specializes in runes and create your own set by writing down the meaning you want each rune to symbolize.

When using runes in modern magic, it is important to keep any negative intentions out of the process because the power of a single rune will be multiplied by all other runes in its set, so use caution when performing this type of magic. Rune magic can be used to bring luck or even banish evil spirits, and it is all up to the user how they choose to use their runes. Rune energies are very powerful, but if you practice using them properly, then you will have no trouble with your magical practice.

RUNE MAGIC IN RUNE INSCRIPTIONS

The most widely practiced form of rune magic today is the use of runes in magical inscriptions. Runes are a system that has been used to pass information and divine intentions for millennia, using symbols for magic dates back as far ago as 2200 BCE (Cuneiform) when they were carved onto birchwood tablets with animal blood. And while these systems may have fallen out of favor over time, it's important to remember their power - which can be harnessed by anyone willing enough through study!

The history behind runes dates back centuries upon centuries; we know about them first appearing on little wooden panels found buried beneath settlements from around 2200 BCE (Before Common Era). These ancient practitioners would carve symbols into pieces of wood using cinnabar ink made from ground-up insects mixed with blood from sacrificed animals. They would then stick their Rune spells onto designated objects for various purposes (like Rune magic talismans, Rune love spells, or Rune money spells.) These inscriptions were used to achieve numerous goals ranging from luck to protection.

RUNE SCRIPTS

Rune scripts are a form of magic created by taking care to carve runes in the right order and design. The runes themselves can be made into a horizontal row to create one basic rune or stacked on top of each other like an arrow-shaped stick figure with their name written vertically under it for convenience's sake. Rune scripts are most commonly used for Rune Money Spells, Rune Love Spells, Rune Protection and Rune Curse Spells. Rune magic is written in a format that is easy to understand and quick to use; the only hard part comes with actually doing it!

The history of Rune Scripts dates back as far as the Norse themselves, who originally practiced it with their Rune Love Spells. Rune Scripts have a long history of Rune Magic practice, and so they're often found in their simplest forms within inscriptions written on early Rune magic talismans for luck or protection.

To separate them from other forms of Rune Magic, Rune Scripts use singular runes that can be further broken down into smaller shapes and designs to form Rune Spells. Rune spells are not super complicated, and they make Rune Magic a lot more user-friendly than some other methods of Rune spellcasting!

A rune script will typically have at least three and no more than nine runes. Even numbers can be used if they resonate with you. However, rune workers who are rooted in Germanic traditional magic normally chose an odd number—either 3, 5, 7, or 9—but there's no reason you can't use even numbers if they connect with you.

The most crucial component is that you carefully evaluated the meanings and magical applications of the selected runes before placing them in the sequence that best depicts your magical aim. Consider the rune script as a way of "telling the story" of what you want to happen. Keep in mind that a talisman with more runes isn't always a more potent amulet. You risk energetically "cluttering" the work if you fill it with more than you need to communicate your intentions successfully.

RUNIC TALISMANS

Runic talismans can also be made to help achieve a specific magical aim, like getting a new job or attracting a new love connection. The runes are carved into a "tine" in this scenario, typically a strip of wood or bark and stone, metal, or even paper if necessary. Carving is the conventional way; however, runes can also be sketched or painted onto a surface to create a talisman, ensuring that any runic shapes are created with sufficient care and attention.

No matter how Rune talismans are created, they're carved to be used as Rune Magic amulets. Rune magic talismans can vary in size; the most popular Rune Magic talismans tend to be small enough that you can wear them around your neck easily or perhaps on a bracelet. They seldom exceed an inch in length so that they can be concealed easily.

Rune talismans are designed to help you achieve Rune Magic energies so that you can get your wish fulfilled in reality! Rune talismans, Rune jewelry and Rune pendants make a perfect addition to Rune charm bracelets or Rune necklaces because they're ready-made Rune spells meant to boost the Rune amulet's power. Rune talismans can be placed in Rune candle magic to enhance the Rune Magic candles' success.

A Rune talisman is created with a focus on your desire. As you handle each rune, envision what you want to manifest as if it were already an accomplished reality, and channel that energy into focusing on the purpose of your Rune talisman. Rune talismans can intensify the Rune Magic energies of their surroundings so that other Rune spells are more effective when placed in a room where a Rune talisman is present. Runes don't bring things to you, but they help organize and channel your magical energy into working on your behalf.

To create your own runic talisman, you'll need a "tine" to carve the runes into, a carving instrument, pigment(s) to color the runes after they're carved, a cloth to wrap the talisman in, and a rope or string, preferably made of natural materials, to wrap around the talisman nine times.

Rune talismans are wrapped with a Rune prayer cord that connects you to the Rune amulet. Rune talismans can be worn in the same way as Rune pendants on a necklace or Rune jewelry, depending upon your Rune Magic aims.

Choose your runes, remembering two key factors. First of all, if you don't pick them yourself, you may not have a personal connection with these Rune energies. Rune talismans work best when they are tailored to suit you, and what you need, invocations to your Rune allies and Rune gods/goddesses as well as Rune incantations can be an important part of your Rune talisman's creation. Second, if anyone else helped you pick the Rune symbols, you may not have full confidence in their efficacy even if they're perfectly acceptable Rune symbols. Rune talismans are personal Rune amulets; be sure to select your own Rune magic symbology.

You can charge your talisman now that it's finished! Hold the object in your hands and concentrate on bringing your power to bear upon this, imbuing it with the energies you desire. You may also charge it by placing it under the full moon or in a crystal grid.

BIND RUNES

A bind rune is a type of runic writing that consists of two or more runes. The written word then becomes "stacked" in one letter on top of another, much like blocks, to create words and sentences. Bind runes are often used as symbols and images instead of their meaning because it can be difficult to understand what they say depending on how many letters make up the symbol being read from left-to-right or right-to-left.

Some claim bind runes are the most effective way to use runic magic, and it's always ideal to keep your workings basic and your intention clear and powerful while using runic magic. A bind rune is thought to be more powerful than the component runes used to create it.

Bind runes can be made in a variety of ways. A traditional bind rune is constructed by stacking a few runes vertically, much like the runes are stacked separately. These bind runes have been seen on weapons, implements, and commemorative runestones throughout history, and they're frequently used as protection spells or tribute sigils. Radial bind runes are circular, frequently with runes that resemble spokes in a wheel or symmetrical in a circular pattern.

You should carefully evaluate and select the runes you incorporate into the bind rune, just as you would with rune scripts. When you're just starting, it's best to keep with just two or three runes so you can get a feel for how they interact visually and energetically. Too many runes, like too many rune scripts, can quickly become counterproductive, making it difficult to discern individual runes within the pattern.

The arrangement of runes is a crucial aspect of spellwork, but what might be more important than the design itself is making sure that your intended purpose for using them in spells has an appropriate central rune.

The most harmonious and aesthetically pleasing arrangements are not always the best for magic; choose wisely if you want to use these powerful symbols as part of your work!

OTHER FORMS OF RUNE MAGIC

The Stadhagaldr, or runic yoga, is a series of exercises intended to be used in place of traditional yoga or as an addition for those who already practice. This form uses the body and posture, not only with intention but also by forming runic formations on its surface, thereby physically embodying rune energy into our physical reality.

Galdr, or sacred singing, is another physical form that uses the enchantment of sound and speech. Galdrs can be performed alone as a way to focus your thoughts on particular issues in your life, or they may also be done with other forms of art such as dancing- which makes for an even more alluring performance!

Galdr has been around since ancient times; it's still used commonly today by certain cultures, including pagan-based religions. The chanting style was often taught orally through stories about gods and heroes while performing rituals at home during celebrations like Samhain (a celebration where we acknowledge our ancestors).

Runic magic is much more than talismans and amulets inscribed with runes. You can make and maintain a rune altar, meditate with runes, and even intone or eat them. Runic magic can be a solitary practice or a style of magic used in conjunction with other forms of magic.

Always approach your runic magic with offerings as well as the reverence, respect, and gratitude that the runes deserve.

CHAPTER 6

THE ELDER FUTHARK: FROM WRITING TO DIVINING SYMBOLS

THE ELDER FUTHARK IN WRITTEN FORM

From the invention of writing, there has been a need to encode and decode messages. Early forms of writing used pictographs and symbols to represent words or ideas. As time progressed, methods were developed using letters from alphabets that are familiar today. However, these alphabets were not always sufficient for every language in use at that time, so different variants evolved, thus creating new symbols that represented sounds or ideas unique to certain languages. These symbols are commonly known as runes. Many cultures have used runes, but they became most prominent during the Viking Age (800-1100 CE) due to their widespread use throughout Europe. Runes are from the Elder Futhark alphabet of symbols used for written communication and divination purposes by the pagan Norse people of northern Europe and Scandinavia between approximately 200 CE to 1300 CE. The Elder Futhark is a word cipher meaning that each symbol represents a sound or letter in the Elder Futhark language, rather than an entire word. Elder Futhark is also known as the "Futhorc" (Old English: [æŋga] futhorc), which means "alphabet or [æŋga] of forts" and was used to represent Proto-Germanic, Old Frisian, Anglo-Saxon, and English. It was widely used in writing letters, messages, and religious scripture. The Elder Futhark scripts were derived from Latin, Greek, and Runic alphabets and developed into different forms called variants or dialects (e.g., Anglo-Saxon runes). Elder Futhark consisted of 24 symbols representing concepts or sounds using a complex magical system by practitioners who probably belonged to secret groups or societies. Elder Futhark was primarily used by the Norse and Anglo-Saxons and other parts of Northern Europe, Scandinavia, and Germany by Germanic tribes such as the Goths. The Elder Futhark inscriptions are commonly found carved onto stones (like gravestones), bones, sticks, metal, wood, or written on parchment (animal skin). The Elder Futhark scripts are composed of straight lines that intersect each other at their ends and angles with a single end stem (also known as t-runes) and triple end stems (also known as p-runes). A variant of the Elder Futhark alphabet became prominent in Scandinavia and is known as the Elder Futhark runes, initially employed in writing, divination, magic, and other purposes of spiritual significance into the 1st century CE but became obsolete by approximately 600 CE after being replaced by Latin. This was because Latin could be written using an alphabet similar to the Elder Futhark but contained more symbols (more letters). Elder Futhark has a short history, and knowledge is limited since few extant manuscripts contain Elder Futhark inscriptions. Its use declined by 1300 CE when Latin became the main language of writing in most of Europe, but it remained in some areas until approximately 1700 CE.

The Elder Futhark is a set of 24 runes borrowed from Old Italic scripts: either a North Italic variant (Etruscan or Raetic alphabets), or the Latin alphabet itself. Today it is used largely by runologists studying the history of writing or documenting works written in runic inscriptions on stone monuments, which were commonly found in Northern Europe.

It was also used throughout Medieval times by skalds or epic poets who were master storytellers during their time, writing about heroic deeds and recording history for future generations. Therefore, it is quite natural that such a simple yet powerful tool could capture their imaginations. The Runes to them were sacred and magical, a potent medium to open the doors of perception.

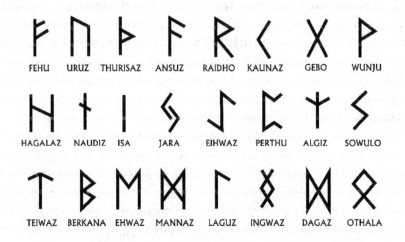

THE ELDER FUTHARK AS MYSTICAL ELEMENTS

The Elder Futhark (pronounced "footh-ark") is made up of 24 symbols and named after the first six runes (Fehu, Uruz, THurisaz, Ansuz, Raidho, Kenaz). However, a closer examination of its structure and makeup reveals the magical nature of the runes as they have always been, long before their transformation into a written script.

To begin with, the names of the runes have real meanings such as "gift" (Gebo), "Sun" (Sowilo), and "water" (Laguz); and are derived from common objects; including cattle, torches, horses, and trees; and natural phenomena; like water, ice, and the Sun. This system of symbols incorporates intangible experiences; such as power, need, and joy; and divine forces; like the gods Tyr and Ing. When used in divination and other forms of magic, however, these names are not always taken literally. Most of the time, the themes linked with the runes are based on metaphors and esoteric connotations.

Runes are a tradition of divination and magic that dates back to the ancient Germanic pagans. When runes were originally used, they may have been interpreted in very different ways than today's approach; for instance, some scholars believe that their magics were more involved with cursing rather than healing or protection spells. This is not exactly surprising given how much our culture has changed since those times! Whatever the runes originally stood for, it is undeniable that runes have immense power. The runes carry with them meanings and magics that we can still tap into today. In fact, runes may be more relevant to some people than they are ever likely to be in their lives.

The 24 runes are separated into three groups of eight runes each: The first group is called the aettir and represents an element or an aspect of nature; they are named after the Asgardian family of deities. This group is represented by runes more directly involved in the natural world (Freya's Aett). The second group referred to as runes of divination or runes of magic, are runes whose powers directly affect the mind and will (Heimdall's Aett). They are associated with specific gods and goddesses from Norse mythology. The third group, runes of the gods and runes of giants, represent natural forces or supernatural powers (Tyr's Aett). The Norse pantheon was made up of various deities representing different aspects of nature, such as war, love, death, and runes. They were worshipped for their power to affect the world we live in; their names gave runes meaning beyond simple divination.

CHAPTER 7

FREYA'S AETT: FORCES OF CREATION

The runes of Freya's Aett refer to what is required for basic survival on Earth, such as food and shelter. They also include communication with other people and the divine that can happen through rune stones or rituals. The final aspect may be hard to decipher. Still, it generally refers to having a full life rather than just surviving in isolation from others, including finding love or happiness among friends and family members too close at hand.

FEHU

Also known as: Fe, Feh, Feoh, Frey
Pronunciation: fey-who
Letter sound: F
Translation: cattle, wealth, money
Keywords: wealth, prosperity, abundance, reward, good health, beginnings

Fehu, the rune of cattle and wealth. Fehu represented for our ancient Germanic people what we would call today "movable" wealth in general - not just cows or other livestock but any material possessions that could be used to provide food and supplies (like sheep). When only so many crops can grow on an acre of land at one time, owning animals was literally what separated comfortable living from starvation.

The most popular interpretation is about riches – a movable property like a cow -- which enabled them to live well or suffer deprivation based on how their communities treated them. Fehu reminds us to appreciate what is going well in our life, regardless of its form. This rune has a broad meaning that refers to prosperity and abundance, including non-monetary aspects such as good health, plenty of food, love and social success, which are vital for having an attitude towards life that will help you be prosperous emotionally and financially.

Fehu is the rune of beginnings; it represents growth and fertility. It is a rune of comfort, luxury and delight after working hard to get something we want. Fehu may represent a challenging time in our life when we need to struggle or fight for what is rightfully ours and self-control over our primal desires and urges. Fehu rules over wealth, property, and cattle.

Fehu reversed is a sign that you are in the midst of an unlucky streak. You could be dealing with disappointment, irritation, and frustration right now for whatever reason. It may also mean canceling your plans because they don't seem to have any positive outcome or meaning at this moment in time despite what was expected beforehand.

Fehu substantially improves your life's productivity and abundance. You can invoke Fehu's energy in your life by chanting it while working or acting in any way that promotes abundance. Inscribe Fehu in gold ink on the inside of your checkbook or on a scrap of paper to put away in your wallet, purse, or wherever you keep your money.

URUZ

Also known as: Ur, Urz
Pronunciation: oo-rooze
Letter sound: U (as in "brute")
Translation: aurochs (wild European ox), brute strength
Keywords: strength, health, power, energy, endurance, creative force

Uruz represents the aurochs, a wild, violent European ox from millennia ago. The aurochs was respected for its raw strength, vitality, and might, but because it was untamable, these qualities—as well as its sharp, deadly horns, which are indicated by the shape of the rune itself—were also cause for prudent care.

Uruz is the rune of strength and power. Our ancestors valued physical fitness as a sign of wealth, prestige and success. Uruz offers us focus, energy, health and strength for our personal growth or professional opportunities when it becomes an integral part of our mindset.

The runes show that you need to keep your body and mind in shape or always work towards bettering yourself no matter what you do for work or pleasure. If you feel run down and tired all the time, it may mean that it is time for a little self-reflection on how important health and fitness are to you.

Uruz is associated with hard work, challenge and competition as well as physical and mental strength. The runes suggest that we need to keep our bodies and minds active through hard work, vigorous exercise and a competitive spirit if we want to stay satisfied and happy.

When Uruz is reversed, it means you are not receiving the benefits of hard work and lack energy. You could be feeling overwhelmed or burnt-out, which can lead to apathy.

You can invoke Uruz's energy in your life by chanting it while working or exercising. Inscribe Uruz in silver ink on the inside of your gym bag. Draw it in red ink on your body to help intensify your strength, especially before and during athletic competition or workout. Trace Uruz on your forehead with your finger to help you find vitality when weak or awareness when tired.

THURISAZ

Also known as: Thurs, Thor
Pronunciation: thoo-ree-sahz
Letter sound: TH (as in "thorn")
Translation: thorn, thorn bush, giant, the god Thor
Keywords: protection, warning, contemplation, decisions, luck

Thurisaz is Thor's rune. Thurisaz is the rune of protection. It foretells defense against danger, or when one's life needs to be preserved through resistance and courage in an unfavorable situation.

Thurisaz reminds us that our safety should not come at any cost; it teaches how we may defend ourselves without sacrificing other aspects of our lives like self-respect or integrity. It is also the rune of self-control and introspection, teaching us to resist temptations that would otherwise compromise ourselves or our goals.

Thurisaz manifests as a shield to block out those who don't belong for you to be safe inside its borders. It also guards against dark forces trying to destroy anything good within its walls by ensuring that only light can enter into any situation Thurizszad helps create or maintain.

Thurisaz can also manifest as the sanctuary itself, sometimes appearing as a protective thorn bush. With this symbol in effect, it is suggested that the protection runes your boundary is now more abrupt, so you will want to consider different methods of establishing your boundaries.

Thurisaz is a rune for decisions in any context. When you cannot choose between two options, Thurisaz can help by making it clear which one is the better path.

Thurisaz reversed shows the danger of watching and waiting instead of acting. This rune suggests that you may be in some sort of predicament and are not sure what to do about it. Agonizing over the situation only contributes to your plight, so waiting and worrying will get you nowhere. It is time to decide and act on it, or something else will have already acted for you.

Thurisaz is one of the most powerful runes; thus, it must be used with caution. It can be used with other runes to boost the effectiveness of spells or bind runes. This rune can be drawn on your forehead to bring amazing energy, and you can also draw numerous occurrences of Thurisaz in succession, directed outward, to help fend against negative energy.

Ansuz

Also known as: Ass, As
Pronunciation: ahn-sooze
Letter sound: A (as in "father")
Translation: a god, ancestral god (sometimes interpreted as Odin)
Keywords: communication, wisdom, divine power, a message from the gods

Ansuz is Odin's rune. Ansuz has a very positive connotation, and its meaning extends beyond that of just one God. It can mean wisdom in general; divine inspiration can come from anywhere — not just one entity. The runes remind us that we are all potentially divinities, capable of having our divine revelations.

Ansuz represents an inspirational message from the gods — a word of advice, wise counsel or instructions. The runes may also bring you messages directly from Odin: runes cast on runes or in a formation called the Vala's dance can reveal their owner's true intent and motivations. Ansuz is often used to encourage or even invent messages to be delivered. For example, runes may suggest that you should create a message and deliver it through divination, or they can simply inspire the message in your mind without you knowing how they came about it.

This rune represents union with your divine source and can be used to connect with spiritual guides, otherworldly beings or even members of your own family who have passed away.

Ansuz is associated with the trickster god Loki and warns you to guard against those who may deceive or lie. Often we are our own worst enemy in this regard since it's easy for us to get swept up by a false sense of security when speaking about ourselves.

Ansuz is often drawn on runes as if in writing; this symbol can bring inspiration when needed most. You may draw Ansuz runes on the floor to attract inspiration as you walk over or around them. You can use Ansuz energy to assist you with breathing exercises that will help you gain mental clarity. Ansuz can also be found in chants and incantations that induce altered states of consciousness, assisting you in finding spiritual awareness.

RAIDHO

Also known as: Reid, Rad
Pronunciation: rye-though
Letter sound: R
Translation: wagon, riding, a vehicle
Keywords: travel, a journey, movement, reunion, changes, a new path

Raidho is an omen of change, and its meaning can range from simple changes within your everyday life to great and confusing shifts in energy around you. This rune suggests that change may be coming in the form of a flood (as opposed to a trickle), one that will wash away everything. It's hard not to feel many things at once when runes speak of change, especially when it's as drastic as this one.

The runes ask you to be open to the idea that everything may be different after whatever changes are about to happen — this can include how you see yourself and what others think of you. For something positive to come out of the situation, try to focus on this rune's most positive meaning.

On a more personal level, the runes may mean that you should take some time off to do something fun or exciting — you'll likely need some excitement after whatever changes are heading your way. It can also encourage spontaneity in relationships and communication as well as increase intimacy between partners.

Raidho encourages you to go on a journey of discovery, whether in your mind or out in the world. It's a rune that can push you out of your comfort zone — sometimes, this may be difficult, but it could also bring positive results. You can use Raidho runes to suggest travel destinations, especially fun places with many opportunities for exploration.

Raidho is associated with the Norns, who are in charge of destiny. If change is headed your way and you're not sure how to react or what to do about it, this rune will give you a sense of what's coming in the form of an omen that will help you prepare mentally for whatever lies ahead.

Raidho, the rune of a journey in reverse, warns that there are problems along your path. The runes may ask you to reevaluate your current situation to find ways to get through difficult times. It can also mean that you should note where you've been to find clues about what's coming down the road.

Raidho stands for a good voyage. Mark Raidho on your vehicle, bags, or even yourself when journeying across long distances, Raidho is a good rune to recite when traveling to bring the gods' favor upon you, and it is an important rune in shamanic traveling for protection.

KENAZ

Also known as: Kano, Ken, Kaun, Kaunan
Pronunciation: kay-nahz
Letter sound: K
Translation: beacon, torch, fire, firebrand
Keywords: light, heat, illumination, breakthrough, creative fire, inspiration

Kenaz is a rune of illumination, carrying the light of knowledge and wisdom. It's associated with runes like Fehu and Uruz, which can also mean financial gain or growth. Kenaz runes are often drawn as an upright spear (which means they may be written down instead of carved in wood). This rune suggests that the message may be harder to grasp than other runes, but it should be paid attention to just the same.

It's not hard to see that Kenaz runes can bring about inspiration and light during dark times — they have a way of spreading hope when nothing else will suffice. For this rune's most positive meaning, look carefully at what you need to see and understand before you can move on — seek enlightenment.

The runes can also tell you to light a fire in your being, as Kenaz runes may suggest motivation or inspiration that's needed to get through a situation. It could be physical energy (maybe you've been feeling lethargic) or mental strength (you may have felt discouraged). As long as the runes are urging you to get through something, this is a reminder that you can do it.

When Kenaz is reversed, it indicates that you are feeling left in the dark spiritually. You may be experiencing a sense of abandonment or isolation from your higher self's inner understanding. This rune may also mean that you are focusing on the things in your life that don't matter while ignoring the ones that do.

When you're studying, creating, or wanting to materialize something in your life, use Kenaz. When you're in unknown territory, whether figuratively or literally, Kenaz can help you "chase the shadows back." Kenaz must be used when thinking about the Law of Attraction or manifesting what one desires.

GEBO

Also known as: Gifu, Gytu
Pronunciation: gay-boo
Letter sound: G (as in "gift")
Translation: gift, hospitality, generosity
Keywords: gift, generosity, friendship, harmony, talents/abilities

Gebo runes are positive runes representing the gift of friendship, goodwill, and new beginnings in life. They're associated with Frigga (the Norse goddess who is kind and generous) and Freyja (a goddess of love). It can represent hopes for prosperity from a trade or exchange and bring about creativity, pregnancy, or a positive pregnancy test.

Gebo runes can also mean that you are bringing about positive change in your life or the lives of those around you, and even if it's hard to see right now, this rune is a sign that things will get better soon. Gebo runes can be very good for healing and helping others, making them a good rune to invoke during times of illness.

The runes will also ask you to consider how your talents and abilities can help others, especially if they are putting those abilities to use to benefit health or prosperity. The runes may also be urging you to share whatever knowledge or wisdom you have acquired with others who need it as well.

Gebo runes can also indicate generosity in the form of gifts or donations to others — whether small or large. If you're faced with a financial burden, look at what you may be able to give up to make some kind of contribution (be it monetary or otherwise).

When Gebo runes are reversed, they indicate that you may be getting a bad exchange or deal, so take care that you're not being taken advantage of. If you are taking advantage of someone else, stop and consider if there's a way to help them without causing yourself harm in the process.

Gebo is a fantastic rune for boosting your ultimate luck. Gebo will improve the overall power and positivity of surrounding runes when combined with other runes, especially in a bind rune. To discover Gebo, to find the X, is to find great wealth and luck, similar to how "X marks the spot" on a treasure map.

WUNJO

Also known as: Wynja, Wyn
Pronunciation: woon-you
Letter sound: W
Translation: joy, pleasure, hope
Keywords: joy, happiness, harmony, bliss, happy relationships, well-being, success

Wunjo runes are positive runes representing bliss, harmony, success, and happiness. They're associated with Frigga (the Norse goddess who is joyous) and Freyr (a god of fertility and prosperity).

This rune can represent the creation of something beautiful or meaningful for you or someone else, as well as a companion or spouse. Wunjo runes can be a good sign for achieving goals, starting relationships and friendships, or making new business connections.

Wunjo runes are also associated with healing and have been used in spells to bring about health, peace of mind, fertility of body and spirit, as well as love.

When Wunjo runes are reversed, they represent something negative in your life. This rune could symbolize a relationship that has ended or someone who used to bring you happiness and joy but now brings only unhappiness. It may also mean that you are feeling overwhelmed by all the demands on your time and resources, and if this is the case, try to prioritize what matters most to you.

Wunjo is a wishing rune that can be utilized to bring happiness into one's life. It is a powerful rune of healing, especially for spiritual or emotional afflictions. To help with depression symptoms, draw Wunjo on your forehead and chant it to brighten your day.

CHAPTER 8

HEIMDALL'S AETT: FORCES OF DISRUPTION AND CHANGE

Heimdall's Aett celebrates the human spirit's persistence in the face of adversity. These runes speak to life's unavoidable events—disruption, change, delayed development, and even unexpected good fortune. They assist us in navigating the more challenging areas of our lives and serve as a reminder that nothing lasts forever. Representing the runes of protection, they associate with Heimdall, the guardian of Asgard and the nine worlds. Heimdall runes are runes that warn you of impending danger or death.

HAGALAZ

Also known as: Hagal, Hagall
Pronunciation: hah-gah-lahz
Letter sound: H
Translation: hail, hailstone
Keywords: destruction, chaos, interference, misfortune, transformation, destruction, interference

Hagalaz runes are runes of destruction and transformation. They can represent something being destroyed or damaged. They're also associated with the concept that life goes through cycles of death, decay, and rebirth. These runes invoke a drastic change to your current situation that may be negative as well as positive — either way, it's a change. For instance, this rune could be symbolic of sudden death or natural disaster in your life.

Hagalaz runes are runes of unfortunate events, but they can also mean something major is coming into your life — whether it's positive or negative, it's big. Hagalaz runes say that you should expect a major change in your life, whatever the outcome may be.

These runes are associated with Loki (a trickster and mischief-maker) and his wife Sigyn (who represents a more maternal side of this rune).

Hagalaz runes mean that something destructive or chaotic is occurring in your life. This may be anything from an illness to a complete lack of money and resources. It could also mean that you are causing unnecessary chaos in your life by harboring negative thoughts and feelings. It's important to try to keep a positive mindset and maybe even speak to someone about what you're going through so that you can figure out a way forward.

Hagalaz has no reversed meaning.

Hagalaz is a potent meditation rune. Sit with this rune to realize that theings might always be worse no matter how bad things are right now. Chant this rune while meditating to help you find hope even in the most dreadful of circumstances.

NAUTHIZ

Also known as: Naud, Naudirz, Not, Nautiz, Nied
Pronunciation: now-theez
Letter sound: N
Translation: need, necessity
Keywords: need, necessity, scarcity, absence, restriction, have patience

Nauthiz runes are runes that encourage you to accept your current situation. They tell you that a lack of something may be for the best instead of having too much of something at one time. These runes symbolize limitations and scarce resources, but they also represent the ability to focus on what is important in life instead of all the things one can't have. They're runes of limitations that can lead you to be more content with what you already have.

Nauthiz runes are runes that help us focus on gratitude and introspection. Instead of focusing on the negative aspects of your life, try to look for all the things you do have in life. If it's a cold winter day, focus on the warm clothes you have and not the fact that it's 28 degrees outside. If you're feeling unappreciated at work, think about what your coworkers do appreciate about you.

Those who identify "Nauthiz reversed" don't see it as the polar opposite of its "upright" meaning but rather as a way to attach some components of the overall meaning to the reversed position. These interpretations can be used for this rune in this place if your intuition tells that a reverse meaning for Nauthiz reversed should be identified. If not, the context supplied by the other runes, as well as the question guiding the reading, can help you figure out what Nauthiz is trying to tell you right then.

Nauthiz can be leveraged magically to empower other runes by acting as an amplifier of other energies. The rune of pure will, Nauthiz, can be employed as such. The runes that follow or surround Nauthiz in a divination or rune reading are the energies that need your attention the most. Read this rune for reflection to help change your mindset when things seem out of control or more difficult than they need to be. Just take a moment to be grateful.

ISA

Also known as: Isaz, Isa, Is, Iss, Isarz

Pronunciation: ee-sah
Letter sound: I (as in "ice")
Translation: ice
Keywords: obstacles, standstill, stagnation, delay, coldness, receiving

Isa runes tell you to be aware of the state of your mental and emotional health. These runes symbolize obstacles in life, a time when things don't seem to be progressing forward at all. Isa runes say it's important not to let this stagnancy negatively affect you or your psyche. If progress is being delayed for some reason, it's important to have a plan of action in place. This way, you can continue your life without getting too discouraged about what seems to be stopping you from succeeding and growing.

Isa runes encourage us not to give up on our goals when we experience obstacles in life. They tell us that sometimes delays aren't negative but can sometimes lead to better outcomes. Holding on to your desire – and not allowing it to be harmed by delays in its fruition – are all that is necessary for your goal's success. Isa runes encourage us not to get discouraged during a delay period, but rather that we should see the positive: at least some good will come out of a blockage. Once you get through it, you can move forward, and the next steps will be a smoother road.

Isa has no reversed meaning.

Isa is a great rune to chant when things get too hot in your life, whether physically or mentally. If your emotional state is too fluid, recite Isa repeatedly to bring stillness and stability to it. Inscribe Isa on your body or chant it to stay cool on a hot day.

JERA

Also known as: Jara, Jeran, Jeraz
Pronunciation: yair-ah
Letter sound: Y (as in "year") (J in Germanic languages)
Translation: year, harvest
Keywords: harvest, reward, natural cycles, fruition, fertility, growth

Jera runes tell you to pay attention to the growth and natural cycles of life. Jera runes let us know that although it may seem like nothing is changing in your life currently, there will come a time when things change for the better. This rune tells us not to give up when times get tough because all our hard work will ultimately pay off.

Jera runes are runes that encourage persistence through any difficulties you may be facing in your life right now. These runes let us know that we should use those difficult times to become stronger and wiser people, so our lives can improve afterward. The lesson is not learned until it is learned once and for all. Until then, there is hope for improvement.

Jera runes help us understand the natural ebb and flow of things in our life; they show us how it's all connected from the smallest elements up to universal forces. This rune tells us not to get discouraged by difficulty or delay as they both happen for a reason and that life moves cyclically. Jera runes tell us to relax and not take things so seriously; that the universe has its way of working out what is needed in our lives. You can't do anything about the present until it's done; you just need to keep moving along.

Jera runes help you focus on the larger cycles of life and their effects on each one of us. If you are trying to make a life decision, this rune encourages you to connect with the forces around you so they can help guide your decision. These runes symbolize patience and persistence, which will allow for much greater rewards in the future.

Jera has no reversed meaning.

Jera is an excellent rune for creating. Jera can help you achieve your goals, whether you're growing plants in your garden or working hard for a promotion. Bring this rune to work with you or scribble it on the backs of garden posts. Remember to work hard alongside Jera's power, no matter how you use it!

EIHWAZ

Also known as: Eoh, Eow, Ihwaz, Iwarz
Pronunciation: eeh-wahz
Letter sound: uncertain (possibly "E" as in "need" or "A" as in "cat")
Translation: yew
Keywords: death, regeneration, rebirth, changes, magic, power

Eihwaz is symbolized by a yew tree. The yew tree is a fascinating example of life and death. It's toxic to people, livestock, and even itself, yet it survives for thousands of years as an evergreen symbol of rebirth.

Eihwaz runes encourage you to let go of the past and embrace your growth. These runes say that if you can move forward from a bad situation without letting it drag you down, it is necessary for your life path. Eihwaz runes symbolize male energy, such as the sun and male mysteries.

Eihwaz runes tell us to be wary of the things we do for personal gain, as they could come with a price. Be careful when you are doing something that may benefit yourself at the cost of others; there may be consequences.

Eihwaz runes are runes that can also help you to connect with nature and all its magic. Eihwaz runes symbolize the magic of nature's way of working out things for the best results in the long run. Nature doesn't always succeed immediately; there are always trials and tribulations, but the process always moves ahead.

This rune has strong associations with runes that represent the elements of fire and water, so if there is an obstacle in your path in life, these runes will help you overcome it.

In addition to its protective properties, Eihwaz runes are runes that also have a blossoming effect. These runes will help you to connect with your inner magic and bring positive things into your life. Eihwaz runes symbolize the soul of Mother Earth and her gifts to us, which can be found in nature or given by the Universe.

Eihwaz has no reversed meaning.

The use of Eihwaz runes is best done when you are thinking about your life path and how it will continue to develop over time. This rune encourages deep thought of the past and present while picturing what the future may hold for you. Eihwaz runes have very little that can be associated with them, but they encourage growth in every aspect of life.

PERTHRO

Also known as: Perdhro, Pertho, Pertra, Perthu
Pronunciation: pair-throh
Letter sound: P
Translation: [unknown]
Keywords: mystery, secrets, revelation, chance, cycles, magic

Perthro runes bring you out of any darkness. These runes show you the way when things seem like they will never get better. Perthro runes symbolize a chalice. This rune is closely related to the runes of Wyrd and Gebo, which represent higher organizations than we can comprehend. Like that of the runes of Wyrd and Gebo, Perthro runes hold deep secrets.

Perthro runes will bring clarity to any situation where you need help. These runes will prevent you from making rash decisions in life that can't be changed later on or may cause major consequences. Use this rune when you feel like giving up on something you cannot control. These runes will help you gain a better perspective on the situation and give you positive energy to move forward instead of feeling stuck in your current position.

Perthro runes may present themselves when things need to be revealed before they can be changed. These runes may be there for you if you want to change your life in a way that will be beneficial for anyone involved. Perthro runes are runes of magic and mystery, so they can help you through any transformations you may be experiencing.

Perthro runes have strong connections to runes like Nauthiz, which represent your ability to see the true meaning of things as well as put order into chaos, as well as runes like Eihwaz, which help you to gain new insight into situations that may require more clarity than what you first thought.

These runes are very positive runes that bring together order and chaos while also providing the results of a cycle at the same time. This rune shows how important it is for people to experience cycles, whether good or bad. This rune is often compared to runes like Dagaz runes, which shows the end of a cycle and can make the best out of it.

When Perthro is reversed, it can signify a negative surprise or discovery. It could also be a sign that you're holding on to a secret that's getting difficult to keep or that you're obsessing over something from the past.

Perthro can help you strengthen your connection to the Unseen World, and you can combine it with Laguz to boost your psychic abilities. Use it to improve your luck, or combine it with Nauthiz to ask the Norns to rewrite your orlog (destiny) in your favor.

ELHAZ

Also known as: Algiz, Eoih, Elgr
Pronunciation: el-hahz
Letter sound: Z
Translation: protection, elk, sedge plant
Keywords: protection, defense, opportunity, intuition, balance

Elhaz runes symbolize a protective mother. This rune will provide safety to those who seek it. Use this rune when you need help with anything. It can be used as protection against any evil forces or bad spirits. It is also helpful in preventing accidents.

The runes of Elhaz can be used to bring back a lost lover as well, although they cannot force love to happen. If you have someone in your life who wants you back, but you don't feel the same way about them, use these runes, and in time, that will change.

They are runes of intuition and guidance. They will help you see the life paths of others, and they can provide you with a vision for your future or help you choose the right path for yourself.

These runes are runes of balance as well. They allow us to find balance in our lives between all aspects, including love, work, family, etc. Like many other runes, the runes of Elhaz will also help you find the balance between dark and light energies.

Elhaz runes hold deep secrets just like runes like Laguz, which represents our ability to tap into this knowledge.

Elhaz reversed could mean that you've been letting your life go by without getting what you want. You may be losing touch with what matters most to you or even doing something pretty stupid and senseless.

Elhaz can be used to defend yourself, your belongings, other people, and pets. Inscribe this on the reverse side of your pet's collar tag to keep them safe. Draw this rune on your forehead to protect yourself in dangerous or unknown situations, and it also makes a great piece of jewelry.

SOWILO

Also known as: Sowulu, Sol, Sunna
Pronunciation: so-we-loh
Letter sound: S
Translation: Sun
Keywords: light, energy, good health, success, mind, consciousness

Sowilo runes signify the Sun. This is because they are runes of great energy and light. They can bring success into your life in many ways and stimulate personal growth as well. Sowilo runes will help you achieve goals, and it represents the sun in our solar system, which could be one reason why health and consciousness are associated with this runic alphabet.

Sowilo runes can give you the energy to overcome any challenges in your life. They will help add that extra spark of motivation when you need it, and sometimes it's just a matter of focusing on the positive. You can use these runes for meditation, personal growth or mental clarity.

The runes of Sowilo are runes of success. They will also help you achieve your goals and bring about prosperity, as well as happiness.

Sowilo runes are runes of the mind. They can improve memory loss, mental illness or weakness from other sources. Use these runes to gain strength in any endeavor that requires intelligence or quick thinking. Also, use Sowilo runes to stimulate your creativity. Sowilo runes will also help spark creativity. This can be in art, music, or even science; it doesn't matter your particular forte.

Sowilo is a rune that symbolizes strength and attack. This is the will that dwells within each of us, and it is this will that will lead us to triumph. When Sowilo is doubled and stacked on itself, the Sun Wheel appears as a powerful shield. This is the lightning bolt that connects the sky and the Earth, and it can be used for both offensive and defensive purposes.

Sowilo has no reversed meaning.

Attack, might, and victory are all represented by the rune Sowilo. Sowilo is a rune that should be significant to anyone who engages in any kind of competition. When chanted repeatedly, Sowilo can bring enormous power, success, and victory.

Chapter 9

Tyr's Aett: Divine Forces and Human Experience

The runes of Tyr's Aett speak to the ancient, powerful forces that shape our lives every day. They represent gods and goddesses who humans and spirits once worshiped in nature like fire or water. These symbols also represent parts of an intricate dance between two worlds: where we know what is happening but cannot see it, such as with luck; and places hidden from us because they exist on a different plane-like the deepest recesses of one's mind--but which nonetheless have power over us all.

The runes of Tyr's Aett represent the cold, harsh realities that people must face in their lives. These runes can be used to bring about fear and dread, but it is also important to realize that the greater power behind these runes also means protection. The runes symbolize both physical power as well as spiritual and mental power.

Tiwaz

Also known as: Teiwaz, Tyr, Tiwar
Pronunciation: tee-wahz
Letter sound: T
Translation: the god Tyr
Keywords: courage, victory, strength, passion, masculine energy

Tiwaz represents the qualities of the god Tyr, who proved his bravery and dedication to the Aesir tribe by sacrificing his right hand to keep Fenrir from harming Odin. The runes of Tiwaz represent protection, and it is typically used for defense rather than inciting fear in enemies.

Tiwaz runes are runes that denote courage, bravery and honor above all else. They will give you the strength to accomplish things that you wouldn't have been able to do before, or they may encourage you to pick up a new hobby that requires great skill, like learning another language. These runes can help you see an entirely new perspective on things and the courage to take the first step towards success.

The runes of Tiwaz are also runes of justice and vengeance, which is why they are often placed on weapons, armor or other items that have to do with battle or power. They are runes of anger, but they are also runes of protection and defense.

Tiwaz represents things that should not be meddled with because the power behind it is great. This rune can be used for protection and offense, depending on how you look at it. It is a rune that will help you achieve your goals, but, at the same time, it will not hesitate to punish those who stand in its path.

Tiwaz runes are runes that carry masculine energy. They can help you overcome fears and anxieties as well as increase your courage in any endeavor. Tiwaz runes will make you stronger, both physically and mentally.

Tiwaz runes represent victory and courage. These runes support endurance in all things, which is the key to success. They also represent justice as well and will help you overcome forces that are devastating your life. Tiwaz runes can bring about protection, but there is a negative side to this rune. It can be used to gain victory over people or situations, which is not necessarily good for everyone's best interest.

A reversed Tiwaz indicates a lack of courage or motivation. The appearance of barriers in your path may dishearten and discourage you, but this is also an opportunity to learn how to overcome adversity by developing the skills necessary for success.

Tiwaz can be used in any fighting circumstance, whether you're practicing martial arts or going to court for a legal matter. Invoke Tiwaz to assist you in achieving victory in any conflict. Before stepping into a fight, chant this rune or inscribe it on any tools you would bring to a competition.

BERKANA

Also known as: Berkano, Bairkan, Beorc, Bjarkan
Pronunciation: bair-kah-nah
Letter sound: B
Translation: birch, birch goddess
Keywords: birth, new beginnings, family, growth, regeneration

Berkana is regarded as the rune of birth and can represent a child's conception, pregnancy or other pleasant family events. This female energy rune should be a promising sign for ladies trying to conceive, but it may also symbolize that they need more patience to do so successfully.

The runes of Berkana will positively influence your life, and they will be runes that promote love, harmony, patience, family life, and fertility. They bring progressiveness into all things; this rune can also help you develop a clearer vision of the future.

This rune represents maternal energy's loving, protective and attentive attributes. Maternal energies are present in the world around us, with their love being one of kindness. These forces work to protect those they guide and ensure that no harm comes to them through all sorts of tribulation.

Berkana is the rune most associated with new beginnings, and this can either be in terms of physical birth or mental transformation. Berkana's meaning typically implies a birthing process for something that does not yet exist.

Berkana inverted denotes constraints and challenges in growth. It's a clear indication that something is impeding your progress or growth.

Berkana is a great rune to work with magic, both for actual fertility and new undertakings. This rune can be drawn on the birth giver's stomach by prospective parents who are having trouble conceiving. You can also chant or intonate the rune while picturing the beginning of whatever you choose while drawing it in the air with your finger or a wand.

EHWAZ

Also known as: Ehwass, Eih, Eoh
Pronunciation: ay-wahz
Letter sound: E ("eh," as in "element")
Translation: horse
Keywords: changes, faith, loyalty, trust, movement, travel, vehicles, physical energy

Ehwaz runes are runes that promote patience in all things. They can be used to help you learn more about magic and runes as well. Though Ehwaz runes may bring a bit of mystery into your life with their unexpected occurrences, they will never lead you astray.

This rune is the symbol of loyalty and trust, as well as a means of transportation. You can use this rune in many ways; you can draw it on your belongings to keep them safe or put the runes in strategic locations when you need to travel. Ehwaz runes have a close connection with horses, and using this rune will enable you to see the bigger picture at any given point.

This rune is associated with equilibrium in life in terms of both physical balance and emotional kind. This is also known as runes for spiritual awakening.

Horses are the only important mode of transportation in the ancient world. Horses can also be used to symbolize travel and freedom, just like how they were integral for nomads on their travels across vast plains. This is why Ehwaz may represent a physical voyage or an internal spiritual journey depending on which interpretation you take into consideration; it could very well signify both!

Ehwaz, in reverse, warns against embarking on a journey now and tells us not to leave our homes because it could be dangerous for our loved ones and us, as there are forces aligned with darkness who would use them to their advantage.

When traveling to other worlds on Yggdrasil, Ehwaz is a vital rune to have. Trancework, journey work, and altered states of consciousness all benefit from it. You can also recite or write Ehwaz to strengthen any partnerships you enter, whether romantic, platonic, legal, or professional.

MANNAZ

Also known as: Madr, Madir, Mann
Pronunciation: mah-nahz
Letter sound: M
Translation: man, mankind, human
Keywords: humanity, the self, support, assistance, intelligence, family, tribe, clan

Mannaz runes are runes that represent the self and one's place in the world. It can also be used as runes for protection.

This rune represents humanity and the characteristics of humankind. Mannaz runes can also work well as runes for guidance or runes to use when you need a helping hand on your journey.

This rune is associated with intelligence and the ability to adapt to any given circumstances. It has a close association with the runes for health, which can also help in situations where you need to develop a viable solution to your problem or predicament at hand.

Mannaz runes are runes that offer you hope and encouragement during times of need. You can also use this rune to attract abundance in your life, whether financial, physical, or spiritual.

If you feel drained of energy and your body feels weak, Mannaz runes will help strengthen your health to continue on the path set for you. If you want to regain a sense of power over your life and destiny, these runes can also help you.

Mannaz runes suggest you find common ground with those around you to form allies who will last for more than just a day. It will also enhance your bonds so that they grow stronger as the years pass by.

Mannaz in the reversed position can indicate loneliness, low self-esteem, and self-preoccupation. You may be out of touch with your inner self and require some "downtime" apart from people to re-establish contact. Alternatively, you may be feeling like an "outcast" as a result of a social issue.

Mannaz can help you tap into more of your potential. Each of us possesses something deeply and intrinsically human, and the world benefits when we share that with others. Invoke Mannaz to assist you in bringing forth that which will benefit the world—and you—whether it's creative endeavors, career ambitions, or simply a means to live to your full potential.

LAGUZ

Also known as: Lagu, Laguz, Lagaz, Logr
Pronunciation: lah-gooze
Letter sound: L
Translation: water
Keywords: water, flow, intuition, the unconscious, psychic ability, the feminine, growth, healing, cleansing

Laguz runes are runes that represent the flow of universal energy. It is also related to water and intuition.

It represents water and all its movements: the oceans, rivers, rain, snow, etc. Laguz runes symbolize natural growth as well as change that manifests in your life through spiritual exploration. When you invoke the runes for growth and change, you may find that your spiritual explorations begin to bear fruit.

Laguz runes are runes related to psychic abilities and your connection to the unconscious. They can help you harness this power and use it to your advantage in everyday life. It is a useful rune to have during difficult decision-making so that you may have better insight to help guide you in the right direction.

Laguz runes represent the feminine aspect of life. Although men and women both have this aspect, it is more pronounced in women. This rune represents fertility, pregnancy, childbirth, and even psychic healing if used for such a purpose.

Laguz runes symbolize the transformation of the spiritual kind. When you apply them to your own life, you will undergo profound changes that affect your spiritual evolution. From a physical standpoint, Laguz runes denote growth, whether it is through aging or recovery from an illness.

Reversed Laguz means an imbalance between two forces: being stuck versus flowing forward with momentum - whether it's through work or relationships. When you get stuck in your career or relationship, the flow becomes more one-sided and reversed. On top of this, when we disregard our intuitive side (by not listening to what others say), there isn't any balance at all, and instead, life just feels stagnant for no good reason.

You can utilize Laguz to help you strengthen your intuition and to calm down your emotions. To boost those powers, draw Laguz on your forehead with your finger and intone the rune while doing so. Laguz is an excellent rune for creativity, and it can also be used to help with writer's block. Laguz aids in the healing of emotions and, like Berkana, can be taken to aid in the healing of the reproductive system and the relief of menstrual discomfort.

INGWAZ

Also known as: Inguz, Enguz, Ing
Pronunciation: eeng-wahz
Letter sound: NG (as in "wing")
Translation: the god Ing (also known as Ingwaz)
Keywords: fertility, male procreative force, channeling energy, completion, safety

Ingwaz is the rune of Ing, a fertility deity. It connects to masculine sexuality and male potency. This symbol brings about all life on Earth while also representing springtime vigor in plant life emerging from winter depths with new growths sprouting everywhere. It signifies self-sacrifice and giving up what you want for others.

The Ingwaz rune is often interpreted as a symbol of procreative energy. It can be seen in many forms, such as the project to raise funds for your business or embarking on an adventure abroad with friends and family.

Ingwaz refers not only to fertility but also to creativity that springs from inner urges like construction projects and commercial ventures, which people worldwide use today. To ensure fertility, one of the runes linked with Ingwaz is Berkana.

The rune meaning for Ingwaz includes creativity, wisdom, and prophecy. Ingwaz represents fertility for livestock, growing crops, and family and grants good luck, good health, and success to you. It also denotes the completion of a project or endeavor.

In the runes, Ingwaz represents life-force energy and sexual potency. It is also known as the rune of a man's testicles, which means fertility on all levels: physical, mental, and spiritual. It's not only associated with the male genitals but also with the ovaries in women.

Ingwaz denotes security and a warm family atmosphere. Your home, as well as everyone in it, is safe. You can relax if you were worried about some kind of threat to your well-being in this regard. At this time, you should feel at ease, prosperous, and satisfied with your life. This is, without a doubt, a rune of good fortune.

Ingwaz has no reverse meaning.

Ingwaz can be used to assist with sexuality and potency issues. It, like Jera and Fehu, can be used successfully in gardening as well as creative undertakings. Invoke Ingwaz for bread, baking, and even beer making because of its relationship with grain.

DAGAZ

Also known as: Daeg, Dags, Dogr
Pronunciation: dah-gahz

Letter sound: D
Translation: day
Keywords: daylight, success, hope, breakthrough, transformation, balance, new beginnings

Dagaz is the rune of creation, growth, and opportunity. It represents a time when all things come into existence from nothingness and are fully formed once more. This is a reflection upon how everything began in the void of Ginnungagap. Dagaz embodies the ability to break through seemingly impossible challenges by leading with willpower and careful planning. Seeing your situation for what it is and accepting that you can do anything great – this is Dagaz.

With Dagaz, you can achieve great things with very little resources. It was the rune of victory to the Norse and Germans, encouraging them to strive for progress despite unfavorable odds. Seeing what you want for yourself and acting upon it, even when circumstances seem too difficult to overcome.

This rune represents an increase, growth, prosperity, strength, excellent health, and general well-being. You can get an unexpectedly positive result on a problem or project you've been working on. As exciting new developments unfold, you are advised to be cheerful and keep your attention on the light.

You may feel an internal movement towards change, and you will be presented with a few options. You can choose to trust your gut instinct or go by the numbers, but either way, it's in your best interest to walk forward with optimism as long as you are feeling positive about what lies ahead.

Although Dagaz is associated with breaking through hindrances, it is also responsible for fading the light. The runes suggest that you will need to deal with an unfortunate situation, though there may be a silver lining, and things are bound to get better soon. A favorable outcome is indeed in your future, but it won't come without some complications along the way.

When this rune appears, timing is everything. You are advised to tread carefully as your choices will significantly impact the outcome of a situation. There could be some emotional instability but try not to let these feelings take over and control you.

Dagaz has no reversed meaning.

Dagaz is an excellent rune to utilize in the beginning or ending a ritual, magical working, or creative effort of any kind. It is a rune that aids in metamorphosis and is excellent for assisting us in transitioning into a better environment, whether physically or mentally.

OTHALA

Also known as: Othalan, Othila, Odal, Odhil, Othel
Pronunciation: oh-thee-lah
Letter sound: O (as in "snow")
Translation: inheritance
Keywords: heritage, tradition, inheritance, ancestral property, family ties, tribal laws, loyalty

Othala is the rune of family and heritage. It represents our values, beliefs, and traditional ways passed down through generations. Othala encourages us to honor the lessons we learn from parents, ancestors or other important individuals in our lives, as well as what we have come to know and love about ourselves. This rune serves as a reminder that we are the culmination of our personal experiences. It is important to understand the history behind who you are today.

This rune fosters an appreciation for our roots – because, without them, we would not be where we are now; Othala is a reminder that our choices have consequences and will shape us into the people we become.

Othala is also a rune of protection, safeguarding our community and supporters and representing stability so that we can anchor ourselves in a structure that will not topple down with time. This rune counsels us to return to the foundation that makes us who we are – it asks us to be true to ourselves, our family and our heritage, as well as to put in the work that will preserve it.

If you find yourself tempted to break free from your past, Othala warns against taking impulsive actions because they may have unforeseeable consequences. Don't hastily abandon what has been built for something unfamiliar – instead, be patient and allow yourself the time to develop a plan of action so that any attempts at new ventures will have a chance at achieving success.

Othala encourages us to apply what we know and believe to make our dreams come true. This rune counsels us not to lose sight of that which has been present all along, as it is the key to reaching our goals and attaining a strong, stable, and secure position.

Reversed Othala often indicates family strife and discord, and this could be due to a divorce or significant rift between members. Inheritance disputes may also arise when one member passes on.

Use Othala when you want to honor your family and ancestors, preserve the past and pass it down to future generations, root yourself in tradition and familiar rhythms, and secure a stable and strong position.

To give runes meaning, you can think about what they represent on a deep level; you can also rely on your intuition to help guide you when reading runes or answering runes questions. If the runes never worked for you before, there is only one thing that you need to do: believe in them! There are many ways of having runes read, but the runes are not there for you to find out what they "mean." They are there to offer insight and knowledge about your path and future. Some runes will show up repeatedly; other runes will start appearing now that you know how to interpret them properly.

When runes come up again and again in readings, there is a lesson to learn. The runes never lie, so they may tell you something that you don't want to hear right now, or it might be something that you already know but haven't accepted. You cannot change what the runes will say; all you can do is accept it for what it is and learn from it.

The runes reflect your mind; they will be the first to show you when there is something off about your psyche or if you are not thinking straight. An example would be if runes keep telling you that someone is lying to you, but for some reason, you don't want to see it; then runes will continue revealing this until you either accept it or you learn your lesson and move on. Sometimes runes will present circumstances that are more complex than they appear. This is when runes can be of great help because they offer an outlook from a different perspective, enabling you to see the situation in a larger context. Runes can help you if you want to get rid of bad habits, overcome fears, or if you are facing a decision that is difficult to make.

CHAPTER 10

RUNE READING: A MYSTICAL SKILL

Rune divination is an ancient art. It goes back to the Nordic people of Northern Europe, whose rune alphabets form one of the oldest known forms of writing.

It was believed that runestones could reveal what the future held for people if they were interpreted correctly. Thus, rune divination is best done by rune readers who have extensive knowledge about runes and understand how to ask questions in a manner in which rune symbols can be answered.

Runes are a powerful tool for divination because they can reveal glimpses of the future or past. But be mindful that anything you read in runes is not set in stone; it's more like looking through an open window and seeing what lays beyond your reach. Rather, runes can provide you with a tableau of the present moment, highlighting the obscure yet decisive factors in your situation. They also offer insight into your life by predicting possible outcomes based on how you act now. Don't let fear prevent you from using these tools as part of your journey towards personal growth and fulfillment.

Furthermore, don't allow your inherent wisdom in discernment to be directly affected by too much dependence on the runes. If you find yourself resorting to the runes every time you need to choose almost anything, you are probably experiencing "oracle abuse." Impose on yourself to consult the runes for very complex issues that you can't resolve independently.

GETTING READY TO READ RUNES

SETTING THE STAGE

There are two things to consider to get the clearest reading: a quiet place for casting runes and a focused mindset. Meditation is key and it's important not to let what happened in these instances affect the result. First take some time for deep breathing meditation (about five minutes) where all other thoughts are suppressed; this will help create a peaceful mood before performing any readings.

You'll need a quiet environment free from distractions like television and arguments as well as enough privacy so no one else can see them if they peek over your shoulder-unless it's someone who knows about divination! The best thing would be find yourself somewhere secluded with just enough light coming through windows to give rune stones a look at them. A lamplight or candle should be just enough. After a while, rune stones will initiate the reading after seeing you've got everything set up.

CHOOSING THE QUESTIONS

What sort of questions might the runes assist you with? The answer is anything and everything. Wherever your curiosity leads, they will show a path to take in order for you to find their meaning. They are able pull pieces from anywhere- past lives or current day situations - that all intersect together as one whole puzzle on what's happening now so any question could be answered within this realm.

There's no limit to what you can ask the runes about in terms of the topic—whether it's about relationships, employment, health difficulties, or anything else, the runes can help. Taking a less direct approach to the problem enables more information to emerge than simply asking for a "yes or no" response.

PREPARING THE READING

In the Germanic tradition, the runes would be cast onto the rune cloth by experienced readers. This rune cloth was then folded to reveal rune stones that had appeared of their own accord. Others preferred to cast rune stones onto a designated surface like a map, another rune stone, or even the palm of one's hand. Other readers, on the other hand, may not use a rune cloth at all. This, like so much else about divination in general, is entirely up to you.

To cast the runes in random, simply scramble the runes in the rune pouch, then remove the number of runes you'll be reading. Alternatively, you can spread them out face-down and swirl them with your fingers. You can shuffle your runes in your cupped hands if they're small enough to fit. To find out which way works best for you, try a few alternative approaches.

BASIC STEPS IN CASTING RUNES

STEP 1: KNOW YOUR RUNES

Each rune has a specific meaning that can be used in conjunction with other runes for better divination. To learn about the runes, review this information found in the preceding chapters. You may also research related topics from reliable sources such as books and manuals published by actual practitioners of divination. Be wary of online materials, as some might be inaccurate.

STEP 2: GATHER YOUR TOOLS

You will need runes, paper, and a pencil. If you want your runes to be customized for divination, then consider investing in runes that have smooth surfaces, so it's easier to read the rune scripts.

A quartz pendulum is great for revealing more information when you are unsure about what rune to choose. However, you can also use runes on their own without the pendulum if you have a good feel for runes and how they work.

STEP 3: CHOOSE RUNES FOR YOUR QUESTION

If your question is very specific, choose only runes that pertain to your query. If it's more general, then consider runes from randomly generated rune combinations.

Listen to your intuition as you choose runes. Let it guide you towards those runes whose messages resonate with the circumstances surrounding your question.

STEP 4: HOLD AND READ EACH RUNE

Take each rune in one hand and press them against the palm of your other hand as you say its name or sound out its letter in the rune script. Hold the runes for a few seconds before reading each rune. Remember that runes can also be placed in front of you, or on top of each other, with the runes' messages being revealed through multiple vantage points.

As you touch the runes on your hands, close your eyes and try to feel them as they "speak" to you in their unique ways. Try to maintain as much of a sense of inner silence as you can to better discern the runes' messages.

If your intuition gives you any feelings while holding runes, follow those feelings! If it's shaking its head in disapproval at something, don't do it or stop whatever actions you are taking that don't feel right to your inner wisdom. Let that sense of intuition be your guide! Feelings are more powerful than thoughts, so remember what you feel when you read runes, as it's very important in discerning runes messages.

STEP 5: CHOOSE THE BEST COMBINATION OF RUNES FOR YOU

You will receive messages from runes that can give insights into your particular circumstances. While runes can give you very specific predictions, some are vague and need to be interpreted.

STEP 6: INTERPRET THE RUNES

While runes tend to speak with one voice, they may also contradict each other because they represent different aspects of a situation. Their messages should never be taken literally; rather, runes provide you with an opportunity to interact with the runes' energies.

STEP 7: TAKE ACTION ON YOUR INSIGHT

Write down all your insights from runes so that you're able to refer back to them at a later time when needed. Be sure to mark which runes gave you each insight and the order in which you received those messages, as it helps confirm that runes are not arbitrary.

STEP 8: REPEAT THE PROCESS

Keep working with runes as you gain more insights into your situation through repetition and practice. However, keep in mind that runes are never a substitute for critical thinking and logical evaluation of your given circumstances. Use runes to support the decisions you make instead of making your decisions from runes.

READING AND INTERPRETING THE RUNE

The Runes were commonly believed to be used for casting lots or rune readings. In the rune readings, rune symbols were interpreted as answers to questions asked by rune readers regularly.

Interpreting rune symbols during rune reading depends on the arrangement of the runes when cast. The order of rune symbols was considered very important, and it was thought that different arrangements would change the symbol's significance because rune divination is all about choosing the right runestones and arranging them properly to discern sensible answers to your questions.

RUNE SPREADS

Rune spreads are patterns that can be laid out on a table or surface, with each rune position representing an important meaning. These spreads range from simple to complicated and vary in the number of runes they include - anywhere from one to several. Always remember your intention for a spread regardless of the number of runes involved. Each rune is to be considered independently and carefully arranged in a meaningful way so that they take on greater significance.

A spread gives direction for understanding what lies ahead by looking at the present scenario from all angles in order to get an idea about how change might occur or where opportunity may be lurking. There are many different types of spreads used depending on which type of information you need as well as complexity level desired (i.e., simple vs complex). The timeframe involved also contributes because some things happen quickly while others can take years- if not lifetimes! When done artfully, this practice offers guidance through any challenge with compassion and clarity.

STEPS IN SPREADING RUNES

STEP 1: MAKE A SPREAD PLAN

Before you begin, it's helpful to review your intentions for the spread. Why are you doing this? How will runes help guide you forward? What do you feel is on the horizon that needs more clarity in order to take appropriate actions? Keep these things close as they're important to consider when arranging runes.

STEP 2: LAY OUT YOUR RUNES

There are some runes that you'll always want to have present since they represent the runes themselves—Dagaz, Hagalaz, and Inguz. These runes can be placed at the far corners of your spread. They represent the runes' energies, symbols and divination process, so they'll always be present to offer insight and perspective.

STEP 3: WORK WITH THE RUNES

Each rune has its own meaning based on their initial sound, which makes runes the most ancient form of alphabet in all of human history. The runes are also considered sacred symbols that possess magical powers known as Magickal Meanings. Each rune should be carefully considered in the overall context of your spread. The runes will tell you everything you need to know, but they won't spell it out for you when read correctly. They can be interpreted through different methods, and each method yields its own results-which is why it's so important to know what you're doing before taking matters into your own hands.

STEP 4: PLACE RUNES AS DESIGNATED ON YOUR SPREAD

Try different rune positions to see what works the best for you. The runes will speak to you based upon their positioning and how they're arranged. Use this opportunity to see how each of the runes interact with others within the spread overall, as well as with one another (this is important).

STEP 5: LET THE RUNES SPEAK TO YOU

Runes can be interpreted in several ways and through any number of spread types. Once your runes are laid out, give yourself time to contemplate what they may mean based on placement-and then let them speak their meanings to you.

Types of Rune Spreads

Wyrd Spread (1 rune)

This method, also known as "Odin's Rune," is fairly self-explanatory: shuffle the runes in their pouch and pull out one rune. Use this spread when you need help making a quick decision or dealing with an unexpected event. It can also be used as a brief self-reflection ritual to begin your day.

You may even carry your selected rune with you during the day as a grounding if you find yourself becoming too wrapped up in unimportant things at work, school, or social gatherings. In this way, the runes assist you in staying in touch with your mystical inner self in the midst of modern life's chaos.

Spread of the Norns (3 runes)

When it comes to perceiving the extent of a situation, the three-rune spread provides more context than one rune, but it still portrays a general view of the concern. The runes placed side by side and are read from left to right. This Norn-inspired method illustrates past, present, and future developments regarding your concern.

The runes are laid out in a neat triangle, each one representing past events that led to the present moment and future possibilities.

The first rune you pull will be placed on the left side of your spread; this symbolizes what has come before and is manifested now. The second rune goes at the top right-hand corner where it represents current events leading up to or being actively created by us as well as potential outcomes if we don't change course soon. Finally, our third rune, positioned on the right side, signifies what might happen should we continue in the current direction or divert our course of action.

THE RUNIC RIVER (5 RUNES)

This five-rune spread is an extension of the typical three-rune timeline of past (1), present (2), and future (3) but emphasizes how every action has consequences. The next rune offers guidance on the course of action to be taken (4) to avoid the negative and improve the positive in the anticipated outcome. If you follow this advice, then it's most likely you'll see some change (5) in your future.

OTHER RUNE SPREADS

- Soul Rune Spread (6 runes)
- World Tree (or Yggdrasil) Spread (9 runes)
- Hamingja (or Hammergeld) Spread (12 runes)
- Soul Journey Spread (18 runes)
- Final Destination Spread (24 runes)
- Multiplicity Spread (30 runes)

There are many other ways to interpret runes, and various spreads to help you do so. One of the most popular spreads is the World Tree, involving nine different runes that represent the realms in Norse mythology, with each rune position signifying energies surrounding you and how these energies interact, much like Yggdrasil.

Rune castings and rune spreads have differences. Predetermined spots in a rune spread reflect distinct components of a whole—different variables in an equation. In this method, you have greater say over where the runes are placed within your reading but relinquish some control to fate by casting them instead. Their position in relation to one another is determined by where they land when cast, as opposed to what spot they're assigned beforehand via spreads. Casting is best suited for those who are experienced rune readers and have establish a great relationship and knowledge of the runes.

Keep in mind this is just a start, and it takes practice to become adept at reading runes. There are many different methods for interpreting runes depending on the type of spread utilized (i.e., runes that represent each day of the week, runes that form patterns, runes that form grids, etc.). The key is to give yourself permission to experiment with runes and runes spreads in order to find what works best for you.

It could take years before rune readers figured out just where to place runes so they would get answers that are true—which is why rune divination is not a skill that rune readers can learn overnight.

CONTINUING THE JOURNEY

The word 'runes' is a modern term derived from an old Anglo-Saxon word 'rún', meaning a mystery. For those who still don't know what runes are, runes are sacred symbols for divination from a higher power (through Tyr and Odin).

We need to understand first that runes are not just markings on a piece of paper or wood; runes are sacred symbols used for our spiritual development as human beings and should always be treated with respect.

The earliest runes were likely invented to write ideographs so that other people can be educated about what dangers, rewards the place has, but also used as a simple and clear writing system for carved stone monuments and other items of everyday use. Futhark inscriptions are found throughout Scandinavia and continental Germany and date from the last centuries BC to as late as the 9th century AD, as early runes had likely lost their importance as a functional script. The greatest concentration of runes is found in Denmark and Sweden.

The runes that we use today were adopted from Scandinavian Elder Futhark, consisting of 24 runes.

There are several ways to use runes for divination and insight. You must know what the rune is asking, why it was cast, how best to answer the question in runes and which type of interpretation method will work best for your needs. Whether you want answers about love matters or career advice, there's an appropriate way to conduct a reading using these ancient symbols from Scandinavia. The most popular methods include casting on parchment paper with ink made from soot mixed with water; drawing them out randomly on clean white paper; or laying them out as tiles face down on a tabletop surface.

Some users also take into consideration the type of day and time the reading is done. Casting them on a Friday, when the god Odin ruled, would be an excellent choice, for instance. The diviner could also look at what rune cast reveals itself in which position in relation to others, an aspect that makes casting runes different. Other divination methods don't take into account the order of symbols in reading, but this one does. It is a very important factor to consider when taking on an interpretation, not only the initial rune from the spread.

The runes are also an excellent tool for divining one's future. They can reveal the road ahead, but only if you know how to interpret them correctly. They will provide insight into your past and present, but only if you are prepared to work with runes in a way that best suits your needs.

If you've never divined before, then runes may be the perfect place to start. They aren't any more difficult than other methods and give the diviner a lot of information about the runes being used.

The intricacies of the runes oppose simplistic, surface interpretations, as you have no doubt realized. Each of these historical symbols contains a depth of meaning that grows in understanding as you gain more experience. Working with runes can become a lifetime adventure. Even the most experienced rune practitioners are aware that there is always more to learn from the runes, as they never reveal all of their mysteries.

So don't be disheartened if you don't see immediate instinctive connections with every Elder Futhark rune (or any other runic alphabet, for that matter). Keep in mind that these mystical connections require time and effort to develop. In this way, meditating on one rune per day can be extremely beneficial.

You can start with Fehu and work your way through the Elder Futhark in order, or you can pull one rune from your pouch each day and let the runes lead you to the one you should focus on for the next 24 hours. Once you've passed through all of the runes, you might want to repeat this exercise to strengthen your relationship with each symbol even more.

The runes are a powerful tool for shaping your magical practice. Let them guide you in drawing one rune from the bag and looking at both its divinatory meaning as well as how it can be used to empower other aspects of spellwork or even daily life!

Consult books, websites, or friends who work with them more often before picking up a new stone. If uncertain about their meanings, they may not feel right when using them after being drawn randomly without knowing what is required beforehand. Runes will tell you if they're suitable by either feeling heavier than usual (negative) or lighter than normal (positive).

Draw two stones out instead of just one - this way, there's an extra chance of getting a positive rune. An example could be runes that are required for spellwork or runes that help with writing the runes themselves.

Don't forget to draw back in runes you once took out - this is good practice and can give you an idea of whether your runes were telling the truth or lies all along. It may also show that runes were lying, and a certain one will have to be removed.

Remember to check runes before each casting. Never use damaged runes or ones that have been dropped - this usually causes bad luck. Never leave runes out in the open as they can get stolen - place them away from prying eyes. Consult with your runes if you think you lost them. You could be surprised to find that you are still carrying runes around.

Don't share runes or their meanings with anyone who isn't serious about magic or the runes - this can cause bad energy between yourself and others. Don't cast runes for anybody who has no idea nor faith in runic divination.

It's essential to pay close attention when interpreting runes because they provide a unique perspective into personal thoughts and feelings. The receiver is completely dependent on the runic wisdom of others to gain understanding from these ancient symbols, which makes it even more important for rune readers to take their responsibility seriously.

You may find yourself drawn to the magical and spiritual traditions of the ancient Germanic people as you become more receptive to the energies of the runes.

The runes can help you discover patterns in your life. If a negative sequence is repeated often, its message should become clear, and you might want to consider how it may be changed or eliminated. An awareness of this pattern leads to proactive responses rather than reactive ones. The runes can give guidance with decision-making and empower you with an inner sense of rightness or direction during those times when you need it most.

Keep a rune divination journal where all runes are drawn in detail. It may also be beneficial to make a small booklet compiling runes you've already drawn and their meanings, as well as runes needed for spellwork or divination purposes. By keeping track of runes and their usages, you'll be able to see runic patterns begin to emerge in the runes that have come your way.

Let the runes accompany you as you continue your journey for knowledge and wisdom, both in yourself and in the world around you, as Odin did for the runes and as he still does today across the nine worlds of Yggdrasil.

A REVIEW WOULD HELP!

I hope you loved this book and found it worth your time. If so, I would be forever grateful if you could leave me a review on Amazon to help other readers find my work. The marketplaces are tough these days - which is why reviews really make a difference for authors like myself who want their published works seen by the masses! It only takes 30 seconds of your time but definitely makes an important impact in helping emerging writers get more attention from potential buyers out there looking for new books to read.

Thank you again for reading my book, happy reviewing!

In case you enjoyed the notions or learned something useful from what I shared, please post an honest review online visiting the following link:

LEAVE A REVIEW HERE:

>> https://swiy.io/RunesReview<<

OR scan the QR code with your phone*:

The above link is made for amazon.com. If you buy the book from other marketplaces, kindly leave us a review by visiting the review page in your respective marketplace. Thank you

Bonus 1: Free Workbook - Value ~~12.99$~~

To help you take some time for yourself and reflect on what actions to take while reading the book, I have prepared a Free Workbook with some key questions to ask yourself and a To Do List which can help you get deeper into the topic of this book. I hope this helps!

VISIT THE FOLLOWING LINK:

>> https://swiy.io/RunesWB<<

OR scan the QR Code with your phone's camera

BONUS 2: FREE BOOK – VALUE $14.99

As a way of saying thank you for downloading this book, I'm offering the eBook *ASATRU FOR BEGINNERS* for FREE.

In *Runes for Beginners*, Melissa Gomes reveals some of the most interesting and secret aspects of how to perform Runes Reading and Runes Casting. You will discover new insights into the magical word of Runes and how to link with them.

Click Below for the Free Gift or Scan the QR Code with your phone

>>https://swiy.io/AsatruFreeBook<<

BONUS 3: FREE AUDIO VERSION OF THIS BOOK

If you love listening to audiobooks on-the-go or would enjoy a narration as you read along, I have great news for you. You can download the audiobook version of **Runes for Beginners** for FREE just by signing up for a FREE 30-day Audible trial!

VISIT THE FOLLOWING LINK:

https://swiy.io/RunesAudio

OR scan the QR code with your phone:

CPSIA information can be obtained
at www.ICGtesting.com
Printed in the USA
LVHW050256310122
709774LV00013B/1748